Women in the Arts

Dorothea Lange

He who neglects the arts when he is young
has lost the past and is dead to the future.

—Sophocles, *Fragments*

Dorothea Lange

Kerry Acker

Introduction by
Congresswoman Betty McCollum
Minnesota, Fourth District
Member, National Council on the Arts

CHELSEA HOUSE
PUBLISHERS
A Haights Cross Communications Company
Philadelphia

CHELSEA HOUSE PUBLISHERS
VP, New Product Development Sally Cheney
Director of Production Kim Shinners
Creative Manager Takeshi Takahashi
Manufacturing Manager Diann Grasse

Staff for DOROTHEA LANGE
Editor Patrick M.N. Stone
Production Editor Megan Emery
Photo Editor Sarah Bloom
Series & Cover Designer Terry Mallon
Layout 21st Century Publishing and Communications, Inc.

A Haights Cross Communications ⚓ Company

www.chelseahouse.com

First Printing

1 3 5 7 9 8 6 4 2

Library of Congress Cataloging-in-Publication Data

Acker, Kerry.
    Dorothea Lange/by Kerry Acker.
        p. cm.—(Women in the arts)
Includes index.
Summary: Discusses the life and work of the twentieth century
American photographer, Dorothea Lange.
    ISBN 0-7910-7460-9 (Hardcover)
    1. Lange, Dorothea—Juvenile literature. 2. Women photographers—
United States—Biography—Juvenile literature. 3. Photographers—
United States—Biography—Juvenile literature. [1. Lange, Dorothea.
2. Photographers. 3. Women—Biography.] I. Title. II. Series: Women
in the arts (Philadelphia, Pa.)
TR140.L3A63 2003
770'.92—dc21
                                                    2003009473

Table of Contents

Introduction

Congresswoman Betty McCollum
Minnesota, Fourth District
Member, National Council on the Arts

I am honored to introduce WOMEN IN THE ARTS, a continuing series of books about courageous, talented women whose work has changed the way we think about art and society. The women highlighted in this series were persistent, successful, and at times controversial. They were unafraid to ask questions or challenge social norms while pursuing their work. They overcame barriers that included discrimination, prejudice, and poverty. The energy, creativity, and perseverance of these strong women changed our world forever.

Art plays a critical role in all our lives, in every culture, and especially in the education of young people. Art can be serious, beautiful, functional, provocative, spiritual, informative, and illuminating. For all of the women in this series, their respective forms of artistic expression were a creative exploration and their professional calling. Their lives and their work transformed the world's perception of a woman's role in society.

In reading this series, I was struck by common themes evident in these women's lives that can provide valuable lessons for today's young women.

One volume tells the story of Coco Chanel, the first fashion designer to create clothing for women that was both attractive and utile. Chanel was one of the first women to run a large, successful business in the fashion industry. Today, it is hard to imagine the controversy Chanel stirred up simply by making women's clothing beautiful, comfortable, and practical. Chanel understood that women wanted a sense of style and professionalism in their fashion, as men had in theirs.

Chanel's extraordinary success demonstrates that we should not be afraid to be controversial. Even today, women of all ages worry far too much about stepping on toes or questioning authority. To make change, in our own lives or in our community, we need to stand up and speak out for our beliefs. The women of this series often defied convention and ruffled some feathers, but they never stopped. Nina Simone sang beautifully, but she also spoke out against the injustice of racism, regardless of how it affected her career.

It is equally important for us women to ask ourselves, "What do I want from my life?" We all struggle to answer this deceptively simple question. It takes courage to answer it honestly, but it takes far more courage to answer the question and then *act* on that answer. For example, Agnes de Mille realized she had "nothing to lose by being direct." She stuck to her vision for *Rodeo,* insisted on the set and composer she envisioned, and eventually produced her ballet—the way she wanted to. She believed in her vision, and the result was a great success. Dorothea Lange, having decided she wanted to become a photographer, asked for photography jobs, even though she had no experience and it was a profession that few women pursued.

In our society, we expect that all people should be treated with respect and dignity, but this has not always been true. Nina Simone faced discrimination and overcame social norms that promoted racial injustice. She confronted prejudice and disrespect directly, sometimes refusing to perform when an audience was unruly or rude. One evening, when she was only eleven years old, she even delayed her performance until her own parents were allowed to sit in the front row—seats that they had been asked to vacate for white people. Her demand for respect took courage.

Women's equality not only benefits women, but also brings a unique perspective to the world. For example, the brilliance of Dorothea Lange's photography was in large part due to her empathy for her subjects. She knew that to tell their story, she needed to earn their trust and to truly understand their lives.

Each of these women used her art to promote social justice. Coco Chanel used her designs to make women's lives easier and more comfortable, while Nina Simone was as committed to civil rights as she was to her music. Dorothea Lange's photographs convinced Washington of the need to establish sanitary camps for migrant families, and Virginia Woolf's writing pushed the question of equal rights for women.

Because the women in these books, and so many others like them, took risks and challenged society, women today have more opportunity than ever before. We have access to equal education, and we are making great strides in the workplace and in government.

As only the second woman from Minnesota ever elected to serve in Congress, I know how important it is to have strong female role models. My grandmothers were born in a time when women did not have the right to vote, but their granddaughter is now a Member of Congress. Their strength, wisdom, and courage inspire me. Other great women, such as Congresswoman Barbara Jordan and Congresswoman Shirley Chisholm, also inspired me with their leadership and determination to overcome gender and racial discrimination to serve in Congress with distinction.

Dorothea Lange once said, "I have learned from everything, and I'm constantly learning." I know that I too am constantly learning. I hope the women in this series will inspire you to learn and to lead with courage and determination. Art, as a profession or a hobby, can be either an expression or an agent of change. We need to continue to encourage women to add their voices to our society through art.

The women profiled in this series broke barriers, followed their hearts, refused to be intimidated, and changed our world. Their lives and successes should be a lesson to women everywhere. In addition, and importantly, they created lasting and meaningful art. I hope that you will enjoy this series as much as I have.

The Supreme Humanist

The camera is an instrument that teaches people how to see without a camera.

— Dorothea Lange, quoted in
The Los Angeles Times, August 13, 1978

Dorothea Lange was exhausted. It was early March of 1936, and she had been on the road for a long, cold month. She was finishing up her first significant trip in the field alone, photographing migrant farm workers throughout California. She had been working diligently, often up to fourteen hours a day. In addition to finding subjects, talking with them, and taking their pictures, Lange also was taking detailed notes for captions, keeping track of money she spent on film and mileage covered, and making sure her camera equipment was clean and operating properly. It was a

The activist with a camera. On the road with camera and film in hand, Lange photographed the lives of migrant workers displaced by the Depression. Her work earned her a job with the Farm Security Administration and eventually would jumpstart her career as one of America's groundbreaking documentary photographers.

rainy and dreary evening, but she was finally making her way back home.

On assignment for the Farm Security Administration (FSA), Lange was documenting the dreadful living conditions of the migrants, a continuation of the work that she had begun earlier with the economist Paul Schuster Taylor (who would eventually become her husband). The Great Depression had disrupted the lives of people across the nation, but American farmers were particularly devastated. Prices for such crops as wheat, corn, and cotton plummeted, along with the cost for livestock, forcing farmers and their families to abandon their homes and search for work elsewhere. The development of more modern agricultural equipment and machinery was driving other farmers out of work. And terrible dust storms had destroyed the topsoil on farms in the Midwest, causing even more farm families to flee. They were all heading to the West, where the land was rich and fertile.

Thousands of migrant workers flooded into California, looking for any agricultural jobs they could find. They moved all around the state, picking fruits and vegetables, barely making enough money to survive and feed their families. They set up makeshift camps, living in huts made of cardboard, tin, canvas, or anything else they could scrape up. They were undernourished, and many of them were sick due to the unsanitary conditions. The migrants were desperately poor, and there appeared to be no relief from their suffering.

The FSA employed Lange to take photographs of this mass migration. The head of the organization had seen the powerful report that Lange and Taylor had prepared while they were working for the state of California, and he was so impressed by her photographs that he hired her immediately. (Lange took the pictures while Taylor compiled facts and wrote analyses. Their study was so compelling that the government set up temporary sanitary camps for the families.)

This assignment, one of her first for the FSA, was an especially grueling one for Lange. She photographed very early in the morning and continued until the sun went down. Lange had seen a lot of misery on this trip, and she was drained. But now she had just seven hours left until she was home.

As she drove along on the empty highway, surrounded in her car by equipment and several rolls of unexposed film, she glimpsed, from the corner of her eye, a sign on the side of the road that read "Pea Pickers' Camp." She continued ahead, not wanting to stop. But as she drove on, she started to have an inner argument. "Dorothea, how about that camp back there? What is the situation back there? Are you going back? Nobody could ask this of you now, could they? To turn back certainly isn't necessary. Haven't you plenty of negatives already on this subject. . . . Besides, if you take a camera out in this rain, you're just asking for trouble. Now, be reasonable." (Partridge, 20)

About twenty miles later, Lange made a U-turn. "I was following instinct, not reason," she said later on. She drove into the camp, where she saw several lean-to tents resting on the bare, soggy ground. There were a few families living in squalor there, yet she spotted one particular woman and approached her "as if drawn by a magnet." The exhausted-looking woman was surrounded by four hungry, dirty children. She didn't ask Lange any questions; she just told her that she was 32 years old and that she and her family had been surviving on the frozen vegetables they scavenged from the field and birds her older children had killed with stones. She was stranded in the dreary, desolate camp because she had just sold her car tires to buy food. Lange later said, "She seemed to know that my pictures might help her, and so she helped me." (Partridge, 20)

Lange spent less than ten minutes with the woman and her kids, making just six exposures, moving closer and closer with each shot. She didn't arrange anything or direct the woman or children at all, relying instead on her intuition and the strong connection she felt to the woman. When she was done photographing the woman and her family, she didn't take any pictures of the other pea pickers. She knew that she had just found the subject she was looking for and fulfilled the essence of her assignment.

When she got up the next morning, she made prints of the photos and immediately went to the city editor of *The San Francisco News*, telling him about the appalling conditions she discovered at the pea pickers' camp in Nipomo. She said that the crop had been ruined and that thousands were starving. On March 10, the *News* ran her story and

THE FSA

The Farm Security Administration (FSA), the government agency that was employing Lange at this time, was part of a larger series of programs sponsored by President Franklin D. Roosevelt to combat the rural poverty of the 1930s. Crop prices had begun to drop at the end of World War I. Throughout the 1920s, farmers had mechanized and had worked the land aggressively to turn a profit on their crops, but their efforts had only driven them into debt and ruined the soil. Also, as cultivated fields replaced the natural grasslands of the South, wind caused erosion; severe drought followed in the early 1930s, and dried-up farms actually began to blow away. President Roosevelt formed the Agricultural Adjustment Administration in 1933 to reduce production and stabilize crop prices, but some of the program's reforms pushed smaller farmers out of business. Many were already losing their land to their creditors, and those ruined by the New Deal swelled the ranks of the sharecroppers.

In 1935, as the situation became alarming, the

used some of her photos, and soon the piece was picked up by newspapers across the country. The government reacted immediately, sending twenty thousand pounds of food to the migrants.

One of the images, which Lange called "Migrant Mother," went on to become not only the most famous photograph produced by the FSA but a true symbol of the Depression. It is one of the most widely reproduced and recognized images in American photography. But it is just one of many profoundly moving and powerful photos taken over the course of Lange's career. In addition to her work for the FSA,

Resettlement Administration (RA) was formed to give loans to individual farmers and to plan communities for the displaced. The RA recorded its work through its Historical Section, employing a number of noted photographers. Its name changed to the Farm Security Administration (FSA) in 1937, when it became a part of the U.S. Department of Agriculture. The FSA established many communities for migrant workers, especially in California, and these were the source of much of Lange's work.

By the early 1940s, the FSA was attracting criticism. California businesses were reluctant to lose a cheap source of labor, and citizens resented the cost of the camps and what they saw as government sponsorship of communism. In response, the FSA's focus shifted to the war, especially after the shocking Pearl Harbor attack of December 7, 1941. The FSA began to lose its budget in 1942, and in that year it was incorporated into the Office of War Information. The Historical Section's photographs were transferred to the Library of Congress in 1944.

"Migrant Mother, Nipomo, California." This captivating photograph was taken in February of 1936 and later exhibited at the Museum of Modern Art in New York City and reproduced elsewhere. "Migrant Mother" became a symbol of the Depression. This single photograph of an unemployed pea picker with her children opened the nation's eyes to the depth of human suffering facing millions of Americans in these "bitter years."

she also made memorable pictures of Japanese-Americans in internment camps during World War II, black tenant farmers, unemployed men on breadlines, and women and children all over the world. Regardless of whom she photographed, Lange created penetrating and insightful portraits that managed to reveal her subjects' suffering *and* their dignity. She aroused such compassion for those she photographed that she was called the "Supreme Humanist." A pioneer in the field of documentary photography, Dorothea Lange remains one of the most admired and beloved American photographers of all time.

The Outsider

1895–1913

The trouble with me is that I'm an outsider. And that's a very hard thing to be in American life.
> —Jacqueline Kennedy Onassis, quoted in *The Unknown Wisdom of Jacqueline Kennedy Onassis*, ed. Bill Adler

In photography, the smallest thing can be a great subject.
> —Photographer Henri Cartier-Bresson

Hoboken, New Jersey, occupying just one square mile of land, sits directly across the Hudson River from lower Manhattan in New York City. In the mid-nineteenth century, the tiny town bustled with activity, serving as a port for ocean liners that carried throngs of European immigrants across the Atlantic Ocean. While many disembarking passengers left to begin their new lives in towns scattered throughout the United States, others, including Dorothea Lange's German grandparents,

Martin and Dorothea, ca. 1905. An early portrait of the
photographer with her younger brother, Henry Martin.
Even at this early age, Lange began to withdraw from her
peers and family; she was embarrassed by the permanent
limp and the muscle atrophy in her right leg that had
resulted from her bout with polio at the age of seven. Her
withdrawn nature, as well as her disability, allowed Lange
later in life to identify with the displaced and destitute
families she photographed during the Great Depression.

decided to stay right in Hoboken. By the time Dorothea was
born in 1895, there were 45,000 people living in the immigrant
town. Half of them were of German descent.

Lange's maternal grandmother, Sophie Vottler, came over

from Stuttgart with her sister, brothers, and mother, Ottelia. Lange's great uncles, who were in their twenties when they made the transatlantic trip, had been trained as printmakers in Germany and quickly established businesses in the United States. Sophie's sister, Carolina, never married and eventually taught seventh-graders. Sophie herself was a dressmaker, and she married Frederick Lange. They had five children—four boys and Joanna ("Joan"), Dorothea's mother.

Joan Lange was 21 years old when she married 25-year-old Heinrich ("Henry") Martin Nutzhorn on May 27, 1894. Henry's parents, Bernhard and Dorothea, were also German immigrants. Henry was a lawyer, with a successful practice in Hoboken. Joan worked as a librarian before wedding Henry, but she also sang soprano in local recitals. The couple rented an attractive brownstone row house at 1041 Bloomfield, a tranquil street a mere block away from the main thorough-fare. This was the house where their first child, Dorothea Margaretta Nutzhorn, was born on May 25, 1895. She was named after her paternal grandmother. (Dorothea later renounced the name Nutzhorn and took her mother's maiden name, Lange.)

"LIMPY"

Six years after Dorothea's birth in 1901, her parents had another child, a boy named Henry Martin. Just a year after his birth, Dorothea experienced a traumatic event that was to change her life forever. The seven-year-old girl was stricken with polio, a dreadful, frightening disease that had no known cure at the time. Lange was in physical pain for days; she had a fever and her whole body ached. When the fever finally broke, she was drained and weakened, and her right leg and foot were permanently damaged. From then on, Lange's foot was inflexible, and her leg was thin and weak. She had to wear two different-sized shoes because her right foot was a half size smaller than her left. And Lange had a limp for the rest of her life.

Young Dorothea was deeply affected by the disease. She could no longer run around, or participate in other physical activities with children her age. Children often teased her, calling her "Limpy." She would attempt to walk as best she could, but she never could get around or play like the other children. To make things even worse, her mother, Joan, was embarrassed by her daughter's disability. Later on in life, Lange remembered how, when she and her mother were out for a stroll and a friend approached them, Joan would whisper to her daughter, "Now walk as well as you can!" Her mother's attitude saddened and embittered Dorothea. She thought Joan was ashamed of her, and she grew to resent her mother's concern for outward appearances.

But as an adult, Dorothea Lange would come to believe that her bout with polio was "perhaps the most important thing that happened to me. It formed me, guided me, instructed me, helped me, and humiliated me. All these things at once. I've never gotten over it, and I am aware of the force and the power of it." (Meltzer, 6) Indeed, Lange's disability set her apart from her peers, and she felt a sense of alienation and not belonging. Yet the pain and shame that resulted from her limp also helped her to develop a tremendous empathy for others suffering from ill fortune. She could understand the plight of those who felt like outsiders because she experienced those feelings herself. And, years later, Lange would say, "When I was working . . . with people who were strangers to me, being disabled gave me an immense advantage. People are kinder to you. It puts you on a different level than if you go into a situation whole and secure." (Meltzer, 7)

FAMILY LIFE

When Dorothea was twelve, she was confronted with yet another calamity. Her father, Henry, suddenly and without explanation, abandoned Joan, Dorothea, and Martin. The event

"Daughter of a Migrant Tennessee Coal Miner." Lange's limp often made her feel like an outsider in her social circles, but she gained a vast empathy from the experience. In later life, she was able to identify with subjects who felt left behind or somehow on the outside of life as a result of the difficult economic climate of the 1930s. She captured the elements of despair and loneliness in the faces of ordinary Americans and poignantly conveyed these emotions to mainstream audiences. This photograph was taken in Sacramento in November of 1936.

affected Dorothea so profoundly that she was unable to speak about it, or about her father for that matter, for the rest of her life. Still, she did retain one vivid memory. She recalled that her father took her to see a performance of William Shakespeare's *A Midsummer Night's Dream* when she was about ten years old. They went to the show in a horse-drawn carriage, but found out that there were no more seats available when they arrived. So Henry lifted her up on his shoulders so she could see the play, and she loved it. "It was a magic thing to do for me, to see that. Magic!" (Partridge, 10)

But Lange never heard from her father after he left the family. He sent neither letters nor money, so Joan was left to support the children alone. Joan, Dorothea, and Martin packed their belongings and moved in with Joan's mother, Sophie (who lived in Hoboken, too), so she could help Joan take care of the family.

Lange's grandmother was a small woman, yet she had a powerful presence. Sophie was strong, moody, and had a ferocious temper. Although Sophie was often difficult to get along with and drank a lot, Lange absorbed much from her grandmother. A gifted dressmaker, Sophie possessed a refined artistic sensibility, something that Lange seems to have inherited from her. Sophie once told her that of all the things in the world, "There was nothing finer than an orange, as a thing." (Meltzer, 5) While Joan required an explanation for what Sophie meant by that, Dorothea instinctively understood exactly what she meant. Another time, when Dorothea was about six, she overheard her grandmother say to her mother, "That girl has line in her head." Lange felt that this meant that she had "the sense very early of what was fine and what was mongrel, what was pure and what was corrupted in things, and in workmanship, and in cool, clean thought about something." (Meltzer, 5)

Sophie's assertive personality contrasted wildly with Joan's reticence and somewhat timid demeanor. Dorothea and Martin nicknamed Joan "the Wuz," as they thought she was "wussy" and afraid to make decisions. Lange disliked how her mother so often deferred to others in positions of authority. "When I had polio," Lange later recalled, "she was that way with the doctors, and although I was a little child, I hated it. She was slightly obsequious to anyone in authority. I never liked it." (Meltzer, 7) And Lange felt that Joan depended too much on her. But she knew her mother to be a compassionate person, and Lange was devoted to her.

THE LOWER EAST SIDE

After the family moved in with Sophie, Joan started working as a librarian. She commuted to a branch of the New York Public Library situated in the Lower East Side of Manhattan. She made about $12 a week, a very respectable sum for that era. Five days a week, Lange boarded the ferry with her mother in the morning and crossed the Hudson to the landing at Christopher Street. The two of them would walk across to the Lower East Side, a neighborhood teeming with thousands of immigrants. The neighborhood was chaotic, colorful, and crowded, and totally unlike relatively quiet Hoboken. There were people speaking Yiddish, Chinese, Italian, Hungarian, and Russian. Different scents infused the streets—garlic mingled with cabbage, pickles, and other foods foreign to Lange. And the area was packed with immigrant kids; at the time, more than half the children in New York City didn't go to school. They were too busy working so their families could survive.

Lange attended seventh and eighth grades at Public School 62, located near the library where her mother worked. The school was well known for its progressive educational ideas and good teachers, but Lange continued to feel like an outsider, lonely and isolated. She was one of a few Gentiles in a school of almost all Jewish children. Although she knew she was smart, Lange felt intimidated. She didn't think that she could keep up with her classmates, who were trying desperately to improve their lot. She later said, "They were too smart for me . . . aggressively smart. And they were hungry after knowledge and achievement." (Ohrm, 2)

But Lange was cultivating her own type of hunger. She couldn't wait until the end of each school day, when she would walk back to the library and pore over books in the staff room. She was supposed to be doing her homework, but instead she spent hours gazing at the pictures in the books. She was beginning to act like a "photographic observer," as she later described. She'd peer out the windows of the staff room, into the tenements around her. She would watch families from cultures unlike her own go about their daily lives. "I could look into all those lives. All of a tradition and a race alien to myself, completely alien, but I watched." (Meltzer, 12)

As her interest in school life was waning, Lange was becoming an increasingly astute and careful observer. She was developing her own ideas about what was beautiful. Once, when she was about fourteen, she and a friend of her mother's were looking out a window. Lange was staring at laundry, white sheets flapping in the breeze against a background of red brick houses and a late-afternoon sky. She said to the woman, "To me, that's beautiful." And the woman replied, "To you, *everything* is beautiful." This sentiment resonated in Lange, for she had always imagined that everyone else saw exactly what she saw. She gradually understood that she had her own distinct way of seeing the world. She said of this episode, "It made me aware that maybe I had eyesight." (Meltzer, 13)

Lange was also honing some other skills that were to come in handy throughout her career as a photographer. Two nights a week, Joan worked the late shift at the library and Dorothea had to make the trek to the ferry back home on her own. Sometimes she would walk south down to the ferry landing at Barclay Street, but she preferred the longer and more interesting walk north to the Christopher Street dock. This journey included the Bowery, a stretch of Manhattan that was known as "Thieves' Highway." The area was notorious for its filth and foul odors, and for the robbers and drunken men who often roamed about. It could be a scary place, especially for a girl of just twelve or thirteen. Lange later said, "I remember how afraid I was each time, never without fear." (Meltzer, 13) Because of her limp, she was unable to walk very quickly. So she developed a technique that enabled her to blend in with the background. She learned to maintain a facial expression that would attract no attention, so no one would look at her. She called this her "cloak of invisibility." She said, "On the Bowery I knew how to step over drunken men. I don't mean that the streets were littered with drunken men, but it was a very common affair. I know how to keep an expression of face that would draw no attention. . . . I have used that my whole life in photographing. I can turn it on and off." (Meltzer, 13)

LANGE IN HIGH SCHOOL

By the time Lange started high school, things at home had taken a turn for the worse. Her grandmother was drinking a lot and arguing with the family. She even slapped Dorothea and her brother when she was feeling especially frazzled. Lange stayed away from home as frequently as possible, but she wasn't especially interested in school, either.

Wadleigh High School for Girls, in Harlem in uptown Manhattan, had a student body quite different from that of Lange's grammar school. Although she was no longer a minority among her classmates, her loneliness persisted. She ultimately remembered Wadleigh as a miserable place.

Lange was often truant. She usually barely passed classes in her major, Latin, yet she received decent grades in her music, art, and English classes. There were, though, a couple of teachers Lange liked, people she believed left an imprint on her. There was an English teacher who introduced her to new poetic styles, and a physics teacher who was very kind and generous to her. Lange never forgot those people who touched her during her troubled adolescence.

And Lange did make one very good friend, someone with

The more interesting way home. The "Thieves' Highway" of the Bowery was part of Lange's route home from school as a young girl. She loved to take this route, for it gave her a chance to hone her skills as an observer and to blend into the background. It was here that Lange developed what she called her "cloak of invisibility," which became an invaluable asset in her photographic career.

whom she'd maintain a lifelong relationship. When she first saw Florence Ahlstrom, called Fronsie, pass by in the hallways, Lange liked the way she swished her petticoat. She and Fronsie would often skip school and walk around New York City together. They'd ramble through Central Park, attend free concerts, and go to exhibits at the Museum of Natural History and the Metropolitan Museum. But, more often, Lange would wander around the city by herself. She was unafraid and became proficient at navigating the streets of Manhattan. She loved to observe and absorb the excitement and energy of the city, preferring the freedom of the streets to the company of her classmates and the dreariness of her family household.

Lange's mother didn't know that her daughter was cutting classes. Dorothea said, "I was essentially neglected, thank God! But very neglected! Not deprived of love, but they just didn't know where I was nor how I was living. . . . I realize how enriched I am through having been on the loose in my formative years." (Meltzer, 18)

When Lange graduated, barely, from Wadleigh in 1913, she declared to her mother, "I want to be a photographer."

LANGE AND ISADORA DUNCAN

As Lange's elementary school years were coming to a close, she witnessed something that profoundly moved her—that she described as "like getting religion . . . an experience that affected me throughout my life." She went to the Metropolitan Opera House in New York City to see Isadora Duncan dance, and she was so captivated by Duncan's performance that she attended many others that December:

> I had never been taken into the upper reaches of human existence before then. . . . It was something unparalleled and unforgettable to many people, not just to myself. But to me it was the greatest thing that ever happened. . . . I still live with that, not as a theatrical performance, but as an extension of human possibility. I saw it there. This woman had a quality that could electrify thousands of people at once. (Meltzer, 14)

She had never owned a camera, but her years of observing the city and watching people aroused in her a desire to take photographs. Indeed, Lange believed that she was essentially self-taught. "I have learned from everything, and I'm constantly learning. It's part curiosity, I think, trying to discover why things happen the way they do, watching everything, my own activities included." (Meltzer, 18)

3

Learning the Craft

1913–1918

As photographs give people an imaginary possession of a past that is unreal, they also help people to take possession of space in which they are insecure.

—Susan Sontag, *On Photography* (1977)

There is nothing worse than a brilliant image of a fuzzy concept.

—Attributed to Ansel Adams

When Lange made known her intention to become a photographer, her mother responded, "But you have to have something to fall back on!" (Meltzer, 22) She insisted that her daughter pursue a practical vocation so she could make a steady living. Dorothea later admitted that she disagreed with this whole premise, feeling that it would interfere with her artistic goals. She said, "I knew it was dangerous to have something to fall back on." (Meltzer, 22) But she was forced to continue with her

A restless spirit. At a time when few women worked outside the home and even fewer pursued professional careers, Lange pressed on toward her dream of becoming a professional photographer. She was used to feeling like an outsider, so the pressures of society to conform to a woman's role did not faze her—and she followed her mission relentlessly and without caring what the world might think of her.

schooling anyway. Dorothea's mother believed that teaching would be Lange's ticket to economic security. So, in 1913, Lange very reluctantly enrolled in the New York Training School for Teachers, which specialized in elementary school education. Located not too far from Wadleigh High School, the college had a student body that was, not surprisingly, made up almost entirely of women.

Lange's wish to become a professional photographer must have baffled her mother, and many of her other family members and peers as well. Only one out of every four women in the United States worked outside the home during

Lange's young adulthood. And those who did work, out of necessity or choice, had very scant options: Most women who sought employment became typists, teachers, or servants. The fact that Lange even considered a career in photography is astounding, especially given the limited representation of women in the field at the time.

But Lange was passionate about pursuing her goal, eager to learn, and intent on acquiring the skills she would need to operate a camera, master technique, develop film, and make prints. She was determined to become a professional, and willing to work for different types of studios and personalities, to do all she could to understand the trade. "I invented my own photographic schooling as I went along," she said, "stumbling into most of it." (Partridge, 17)

And that's exactly how she landed her first position with a photography studio. One day during the summer, Lange was strolling along Fifth Avenue in Manhattan when she noticed a striking collection of portrait photographs hung in a display window. She had arrived at 562 Fifth Avenue, the studio of Arnold Genthe, a rather well known and respected photographer. Lange boldly walked upstairs and asked Genthe for a job. Something about her must have impressed him, for he immediately hired Lange, who had no training in photography whatsoever, as an apprentice.

ARNOLD GENTHE'S STUDIO

In working for Arnold Genthe, Lange essentially was learning from one of the best in the field. The German-born aristocrat had moved his business from San Francisco, where he'd run a highly successful portrait studio. Genthe earned his reputation largely from his turn-of-the-century street photographs of the Chinatown section of San Francisco and of his shots of the devastation following the 1906 San Francisco earthquake and fire, yet his portrait business was his bread and butter. He'd had an impressive clientele on the West Coast; society families, musicians, actors, and writers all sat for him. But when he moved to New York City, his business grew even more. Genthe's roster of subjects expanded to include such luminaries as the actresses Mary Pickford and Sarah Bernhardt, Presidents Roosevelt, Taft, and Wilson, and the writer Edna St. Vincent Millay.

Every day after school Lange ventured to Genthe's studio, frequently working late into the evenings. She was the youngest of three women on his studio staff, and she earned about $15 a week—a respectable salary for the time. Lange often handled receptionist duties, but she made proofs and mounted and framed the images as well. She also learned such crucial tasks as spotting—hiding the tiny white spots on the negatives left by bits of dust. And she retouched negatives, using an etching knife to modify features on the subjects.

The studio introduced Lange to a totally new and exciting world. In stark contrast to her Hoboken upbringing and the crowded streets of the Lower East Side, Genthe's studio was filled with gorgeous Oriental rugs, fine art, and exquisitely beautiful objects, and Lange found herself surrounded by people of money, power, and influence. Working among such types provided a "look into a world I hadn't seen, a world of privilege, command of what seemed to me the most miraculous kind of living—... very luxurious, everything of the highest expression." (Meltzer, 24; Partridge, 18) Lange was receiving an excellent education in how to do business with high-profile customers, something that would prove to be very helpful to her when she ran her own studio.

Although Lange absorbed a great deal during her period with Arnold Genthe, she later claimed that most of what she learned wasn't photography. By the time Genthe hired her, he had already completed what is now considered his finest work—the San Francisco street photographs. In New York City, Lange said, Genthe was "working within a good commercial formula and making a lot of money."

Arnold Genthe. **The prominent New York City photographer Arnold Genthe was the first to recognize Lange's gift for photography. Although she had no experience, Genthe saw raw talent and passion in Lange and hired her on the spot. As an apprentice in his studio, Lange got her first taste of the technical and business aspects of the photographic industry.**

(Ohrm, 25) Genthe showed her how to tackle the pragmatic aspects of operating a successful portrait studio. And Genthe gave her something else, too—to demonstrate his appreciation for her assistance, he gave Lange what was probably her first camera.

Lange was convinced by this time that teaching was simply not for her. She came to this final realization soon after an unfortunate incident that occurred in her classroom while she was student teaching fifth-graders. One day her students, clearly clued in to the fact that she lacked the ability to control them, walked over to the window and climbed down the fire escape to the schoolyard below. When her supervisor entered the classroom, Lange was in tears. A few days later, Lange confronted her mother and told her that she was unwilling to continue with school, and then she quit the teaching program. Joan had to accept Lange's decision.

MORE MENTORS

Lange soon left Genthe's studio, thirsty for even more experiences and mentors. Her next employer was Aram Kazanjian, an Armenian portrait photographer who ran a large studio on 57th Street. Like Genthe, Kazanjian photographed wealthy and famous subjects, like the vocalist Enrico Caruso and the esteemed Barrymore family. While she was working for Kazanjian, Lange continued to gain invaluable lessons in running a portrait photography business. Most notably, she learned how to solicit customers. She'd call prospective clients and follow a very specific protocol to win them over. Additionally, Lange handled retouching and printing for Kazanjian. Later on, she remembered one incident that stood out in her memory. It involved a photograph of a woman from the wealthy DuPont family. The woman was photo-graphed surrounded by her grandchildren, and she held a large book in her lap that was supposed to be the family Bible. The book in the photograph was actually a telephone directory, and Lange had to manipulate the picture to make the book look like a Bible.

Lange worked for Kazanjian for a total of about six months, yet she still hadn't any experience using a big camera. So she left his studio and found work in the Fifth Avenue studio of Mrs. A. Spencer-Beatty. In this job, for which Lange was paid $12 weekly, she started out doing simple tasks. The nature of Lange's duties changed drastically, though, when Spencer-Beatty found herself in a bit of a jam. Spencer-Beatty had just one camera operator on staff (she contracted out the retouching and printing). Shortly after Lange began working for her, Spencer-Beatty's operator quit. Faced with an expensive commission to fulfill, the desperate Spencer-Beatty assigned the job to Lange, sending her out to photograph the rich Irving Brokaw family.

> It was the first big job I ever did. . . . But I had enough insight by that time to know how professionals behaved on these jobs. I was scared to death . . . not scared of the people, but that I wouldn't be able to do the pictures that would be acceptable to them, hard-boiled pictures, the formal, conventional portrait. There I was, this obscure little piece, with a great big 8 x 10 camera . . . but I did it! It was sheer luck and maybe gall. (Meltzer, 26)

Lange's first foray into professional photography was a success. Everyone agreed that her portraits of the family were excellent. Her career as a portrait photographer had begun, and Spencer-Beatty sent her out on several more assignments.

During these formative years in New York City, Lange picked up advice and insights from other photographers she befriended. She described some of them as "lovable old hacks. . . . unimportant people from anyone else's point of view." (Ohrm, 4) Charles Davis, who photographed actors, society folk, and opera singers, met Lange after his glory years. By the time he and Lange became friends, he was a "broken-down fellow" (Meltzer, 27) with a studio above a saloon, struggling to recapture the success he had lost. From Davis, Lange learned about posing subjects. Davis would position the sitter in front of a posh, elaborate background, often with heavy drapery and ornate furniture, and he'd set the subject's face carefully, exactly where he wanted it, then position each finger. Sometimes he would spend up to two hours trying to achieve just the right pose. With Davis, as with some other of her teachers, Lange was also figuring out what *not* to do. She felt that his portraits all looked exactly alike, that they lacked character. She thought his photographs were "perfect, and completely empty." (Meltzer, 27)

SECESSION AND PICTORIALISM

Throughout this period, photography was undergoing a kind of renaissance. Lange was reading and hearing about photographers who were seeking to transform the entire way in which photography was perceived. A group of mostly American photographers, organized by Alfred Stieglitz in 1902 and calling themselves the Photo-Secession, rejected the conventions that previously had confined photography to a limited formula. They wanted to establish a new definition for photography and to raise it into the realm of fine art. Prior to this movement, photography was viewed as simply a mechanical way of keeping a visual record. But the new photographers, including Edward Steichen and Gertrude Kasebier, wanted to bring more artistic elements to the medium. Some of them incorporated tenets of Pictorialism—they applied techniques to their photographs that were similar to the techniques that painters used in their work. They'd use a soft focus and special printing processes to achieve a "painterly" effect. But most of the group eventually rejected such manipulations and veered away from the Pictorialist aesthetic, opting instead to rely not on equipment or technique but on their own distinct visions.

Another of Lange's mentors came to her under strange circumstances—he literally arrived at her doorstep. One day an old traveling photographer came to the door at her mother's house, offering to snap some shots of her family. They started talking, and Lange discovered that he had no place to develop his pictures. So the two of them turned an abandoned chicken coop in her backyard into a darkroom. They cleared the area of old feathers and chicken droppings, and hung heavy black paper on the walls to keep out the light. They became friends, and Lange learned that he had traveled all around Europe, selling both his postcard-sized portraits and large tinted ones. He taught her how to develop photographs in the darkroom, and he also gave her a rack, used for drying wet negatives, from Italy. In this unexpected guest (she never named him in any of her interviews or writings), Lange found another instructor, one who introduced her to some useful, though probably old-fashioned, techniques that surely helped her along the way.

CLARENCE WHITE

In February of 1917, Lange attended a photography course at Columbia University, taught by Clarence White, a member of the Photo-Secession, whose work by that time had been exhibited at almost every major photography show. White had taught in New York since he moved there in 1906, and Lange remembered him as a great teacher. Although she described him as "an inarticulate man, almost dumb" (Meltzer, 30), Lange felt that he had a clear, absolute sense of beauty. Her experience with White was markedly different from her experiences with the commercial photographers. "I don't think he mentioned technique once, how it's done, or shortcuts, or photographic manipulations. It was to him a natural instrument and I supposed he approached it something like a musical instrument which you do the best you can with when it's in your hands. . . . He had an uncanny gift of touching people's lives, and they didn't forget it." (Ohrm, 7) Lange gleaned invaluable lessons just from witnessing White's instinctual approach to his work.

But Lange later said that she had no designs on becoming an "artist." "To be an Artist was something that to me was unimportant and I really didn't know what it meant." (Ohrm, 7) Her focus at the time was strictly on portrait photography. "It was a good trade, I thought, one I could do. It was a choice. I picked it. But I never picked the role of artist." (Meltzer, 31)

So when her class with White ended, Lange bought a large camera and two lenses and, for the first time, began to take her own portraits in earnest. She photographed her family and other people she knew—friends and acquaintances, and many, many children. She worked rigorously, often persisting all day and night, but she still had her fear. She never felt entirely comfortable in the darkroom, and she constantly worried that she'd make a mistake. She later said that she was "terrified to develop [her photographs]. The fear of failure, those darkroom terrors—they still remain. It's a gambler's game, photography." (Meltzer, 32) But she loved the game.

By the end of 1917, Lange believed that she had attained the skills she needed to support herself completely as a photographer. She had a solid command of the business side of running a studio, knew how to find customers, and had developed an ability to relate to her subjects. But she knew she had to get away to really prove herself. "Not that I was bitterly unhappy at home, or doing what I was doing. But it was a matter of really testing yourself out." (Partridge, 20)

So Dorothea Lange, 22 years old, decided that she was ready for a big change. She and her childhood friend Fronsie were convinced that they could make their way around the world, finding employment in their respective trades

Clarence H. White, "The Mirror" (1912). This is a work by one of Lange's early mentors. White was the sort of man who worked best when he was creating art, not explaining it. Following him to shoots and watching him work, Lange learned valuable lessons on how to capture a subject without imposing or making the subject feel uncomfortable. In her own work, she helped her subjects to feel at ease; it was only in this way that she could capture their uniqueness.

(Lange would photograph people, and Fronsie, who had been a clerk for Western Union, would find similar work abroad). So in January of 1918, the two friends pooled together their money ($140 in all) and set out for their trip around the world. First they traveled by boat to New Orleans, and then they headed west by train, stopping in Texas and New Mexico. On May 18, they arrived in San Francisco and checked in at the YWCA. They went into their room, counted their money, and then left to go out to eat. At the cafeteria, when they reached into Fronsie's purse to retrieve some money to pay for their meal, they discovered that almost all of their money had been stolen. Between them, they had a little over $4. They decided to stay there and find jobs right in California.

Portrait Photographer

1918–1929

It takes a lot of imagination to be a good photographer. You need less imagination to be a painter, because you can invent things. But in photography everything is so ordinary; it takes a lot of looking before you learn to see the ordinary.

—British photographer David Bailey,
quoted in *Face*, December 1984

The day after Fronsie and Lange were robbed of most of their cash, both of them found work. Fronsie took a position at Western Union sending telegrams, and Lange landed a job at the photo-finishing counter at Marsh's department store. Lange actually preferred this arrangement to employment in a studio, as she "wanted to sense the life of the city." (Ohrm, 10) She was hoping to interact with the people of San Francisco, a city that appeared to embrace the artists and individualistic types that populated it.

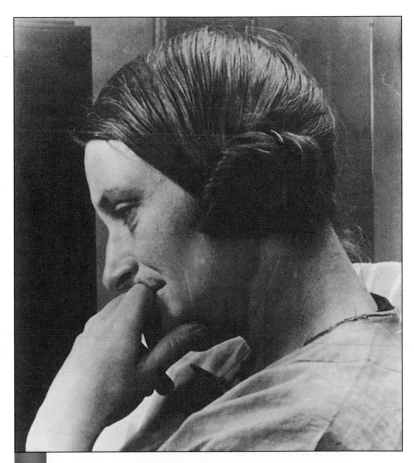

Lange in the 1920s. "No subject can hold for a long time anything that is false for them. It can't be done. You can try, but it's ghastly." Believing photography to be the intersection of what the photographer wanted to take and what the subject wanted to give, Lange captured the true nature of her subjects—including herself. Her passion for the raw, unadulterated expressions of people and places drove her to create some of the most compelling photographic images of her time.

And she did. Lange almost immediately became immersed in the thriving arts community there. On the very first day of her job, she met Roi Partridge, an etcher, and his wife, Imogen Cunningham, a photographer. The two of them and their extended group of friends were integral figures in San Francisco's free-spirited bohemian scene. Lange recalled these people as "free and easy. They were people who lived according to their own standards and did what they wanted to do in a way they wanted to do it." (Meltzer, 56)

Roi had just started working for an advertising agency, and the company occasionally asked Imogen to take photos of some of their billboards. Roi often would take the film to Marsh's to be developed, and one day he started talking with the new girl behind the counter, who clearly knew a lot about photography. Lange went on to cultivate a lifelong friendship with Roi and Imogen, and they introduced her to many others in their lively and artistic circle of friends. Lange also decided to join a camera club, specifically because she needed access to a darkroom. Through the club, she met other contacts and friends, including Consuelo Kanaga, who was a photographer for *The San Francisco News*, and also a man named Sidney Franklin.

Franklin, a wealthy young investor, offered Lange assistance in setting up her portrait photography business. Lange, thrilled and eager to open her own studio, gladly accepted his help. She searched around for a good location and soon found one that perfectly suited her. Situated at 540 Sutter Street, it was a lovely spot, complete with a courtyard and fountain. Lange's rented space consisted of a large, open room with a fireplace and French doors, and a downstairs area where she would build a darkroom.

Lange's good fortune continued when she and Fronsie became acquainted with a wealthy Irishman named Jack Boumphrey who took a liking to them both. He offered Lange a loan of $3,000 to help her in starting her business. She couldn't refuse, and she and Franklin severed their contract without ado. Under the new arrangement with Boumphrey, Dorothea would pay him back the money she borrowed; but she wouldn't have to share income from her business, as she would have had to with Franklin. Boumphrey was yet another example of someone who was immediately enchanted by Dorothea (like Arnold Genthe and others), going so far as to lend her money without really knowing her. As Lange's son Dan later wrote, "He didn't care that she was young and inexperienced, only that she was rare and remarkable." (Partridge, 163)

THE STUDIO

The new tenant went straight to work preparing her studio for business. She purchased a big, dark velvet plush sofa filled with soft pillows and placed it in front of the fireplace. She set a phonograph on a nearby table next to a large stack of records. She hired an elegant young assistant to help her out with everything from secretarial duties to retouching negatives to serving cookies and tea. And she also did something that emphatically asserted the beginning of a new phase in her life: she gave up her father's surname, Nutzhorn, and adopted her mother's maiden name, Lange. (Her mother had divorced Dorothea's father in 1919.) None of her new friends knew that she'd ever been named Nutzhorn.

Almost immediately Lange's business prospered. She started to photograph some of the most prominent personalities and families in the city. Many people who visited the Hill-Tollerton Print Gallery (located right next door to her studio) wandered around the building and noticed Lange's work. Impressed by her portraits, they'd walk into her studio and request to have their own photographs taken. Her clients were very pleased with the results, and word spread throughout the city and Bay Area.

Most of Lange's clients weren't celebrities or performers (as many of her previous employers' clients had been). Rather, they were what she called "the San Francisco merchant princes." "People who came into that building and bought original etchings and original prints were the kind of people who, if your work had any quality, would notice it." She described them as being from "large families who knew each other, and had a very strong community sense and that warm responsive love for many things—children and education and buildings and pictures, music, philanthropy." (Ohrm, 11)

Lange's sitters must have appreciated her singular style of working. She would meet with each of her subjects, often a few times, to try to get to know them and somehow connect with them. She'd attempt to engage them by asking questions and creating an atmosphere that allowed them to feel comfortable. Then when she was ready to shoot, she'd set up soft, subtle lighting. Unlike many of her contemporaries (including some of her former employers and informal instructors), she didn't drape her sitters or use strong lighting. She wanted her subjects to look natural, so she avoided dramatic and theatrical props.

In fact, most of her work from this period showed no background at all. Lange concentrated mainly on the face, especially the sitter's eyes. Her portraits would frequently feature just the subject's head, and sometimes the shoulders. Lange was working with a cumbersome 8-by-10-inch camera then, so every shot had to be taken slowly and carefully. The camera demanded the patience of the photographer and the sitter, but Lange felt that this made for a more intimate portrait. She said, "No subject can hold for a long time anything that is false for them. It can't be done. You can try, but it's ghastly. You have to wait until certain decisions are made: first by the subject—what he's going to give to the camera, and then by the photographer—what he's going to choose to take." (Meltzer, 49)

Lange has said that during this time she wasn't trying to do anything groundbreaking. She considered her photography at the studio to be a practical job. She just did what she could to make her work as good as it could be. To her that meant

Lange's portraits. This image, which Lange created in the 1920s, illustrates the work of her early studio period. Her technique differed significantly from that of more established photographers—it was based less on Lange's own goals than on her subject's comfort level. Lange went to great lengths to put her sitters at ease in order to avoid all theatrical elements and to capture them in a natural way. Her emphasis on the sitter's eyes would become characteristic of her portrait photographs.

"being useful, filling a need, really pleasing the people for whom I was working. . . . My personal interpretation was second to the need of the other fellow." (Meltzer, 49)

All of her portraiture at the time was done on commission; Lange did no personal photography for years. She said, "People like Imogen Cunningham, whom I knew very well by that time, worked for name and prestige, and sent to exhibits. But I was a tradesman. At least I so regarded myself." Lange thought of herself as a "professional photographer who had a product that was more honest, more truthful, and in some ways more charming. At any rate, there was no false front to it. I seriously tried, with every person I photographed, to reveal them as closely as I could." (Meltzer, 49)

Although Lange shot some of her sitters in their homes around the Bay Area, most of her time was spent in the studio. She worked day and night, and occasionally throughout weekends. And the studio was also the focal point of Lange's social life. Soon after she opened her business there, it evolved into a meeting place for friends and all kinds of artists and bohemian types. "That place was my life," she said. Every day at five o'clock, people would drop by and drink tea from the coal-heated samovar and eat teacakes. Playwrights, writers, musicians, and others filled her studio with lively discussions about art and politics as jazz music played on the phonograph.

One night while she was downstairs working in her studio darkroom, she heard some "very peculiar sharp clicking footsteps." "For a while I was very much afraid of those footsteps," Lange said, "and when I heard them I wouldn't go upstairs." (Partridge, 25) She soon found out that those steps belonged to the Western wilderness painter Maynard Dixon, a friend of Roi Partridge and Imogen Cunningham.

Dixon was a popular character who loomed large in the San Francisco bohemian crowd. Decked out in his signature outfit of Western clothing and finely crafted cowboy boots, and often smoking his kinnikinnick (rolled cigarettes of manzanita bark, pipe tobacco, and sagebrush), Dixon was awfully intriguing to Lange. He was charismatic and famous for his colorful stories of Western lore—including tales of posses and stagecoach robbers and Native American raids. He also was articulate, highly individualistic, and had a great sense of humor, reflected in the caricatures and sketches he made for many friends. Lange once said of him, "He was the kind legends cluster about, without his making any particular effort." (Meltzer, 52) The two fell in love, and six months later, on March 21, 1920, they were wed in her studio. Lange's friend Fronsie served as the maid of honor, and Roi was the best man. Dixon was 45 years old; Lange was 24.

LIFE WITH MAYNARD DIXON

They rented a small house on Russian Hill, situated between their two studios. The little house was reached by climbing up a flight of stairs and walking along a brick walk surrounded by daisies, nasturtiums, and geraniums. The rent was cheap, so Lange could pay back the loan for her studio, and Dixon could pay alimony to his ex-wife and also help support his daughter from that marriage, Constance.

Dixon often went away for long stretches of time to sketch and paint his big, sweeping canvases of rugged mountains and desert landscapes. He would also visit many of his friends on these trips—the cattlemen and Native Americans he often included in his art. In the beginning of their marriage, Lange accompanied him on a few of the sketching trips.

In the summer of 1922, the couple traveled to the Navajo reservation in Arizona. While he sketched, Lange went out and took some photographs. This was one of her first photographic journeys outside her studio. She was thrilled with the colors and the vastness of the West. She said later, "We went into a country which was endless and timeless, and way off from the pressures that I thought were part of life. The earth and the heavens, even the change of seasons, I'd never really experienced until that time. Then I became aware." (Partridge, 106)

The following summer, in 1923, Lange and Dixon took another trip, this time to Navajo and Hopi country. They had been invited by Anita Baldwin McClaughrey, who was a millionaire and a collector of Dixon's paintings. Lange and Dixon didn't have to supply a cent—all expenses were paid by Anita. They camped at the base of the Walpi mesa. Anita, intending to compose an opera about Native American life,

MAYNARD DIXON

Dixon, born in California in 1875, was a self-taught artist who started drawing at a very young age. As a child, he used to take camping trips to the Southwest, where he developed a lifelong interest in and friendships with the rapidly vanishing American Indian tribes. His work was influenced by Frederic Remington, one of the most prolific and best-known illustrators of the Old West. When Lange met him, Maynard was designing billboards for an advertising firm, Foster and Kleiser (where Roi Partridge also was employed), mostly to pay the bills. He also was illustrating Western-themed subjects for such popular journals as *Harper's Weekly*, *Scribner's*, and *McClure's*. But by the time he and Lange were married, he was determined to be a full-time painter, not an illustrator. The two made a fascinating, colorful couple. He was tall and walked with a cane; she was short and wore heavy, "primitive" silver jewelry. She also often wore long skirts, perhaps to hide her limp. She admired him and his work greatly; his dedication to his art and his populist sensibilities surely rubbed off on Lange. She once said, "I have never watched any person's life as closely as I watched his, what it held, how he lived it." (Meltzer, 55) studied their music while Dixon painted and Lange took photographs. One of Lange's images from around that time, "Hopi Indian", New Mexico, c. 1923, shows the face of a Native American in extreme close-up. His large pores, shiny, sun-worn skin, and deeply carved wrinkles bring the viewer right into his world. Lange stayed in the area for about a month, but Dixon remained for about four months.

In the beginning of their marriage, Lange and Dixon each maintained their own separate studios, and continued to enjoy their active social lives. But there were some difficulties, one of which was Lange's relationship with Constance (called Consie). Consie, who was ten years old when her father married Lange, lived with the newlyweds while her mother was going through rehabilitation for her alcoholism. She and Lange had problems from the beginning, and Dixon left the care of his daughter totally in Lange's hands. Consie must have suffered a lot during her early life, as her mother was ailing and her father totally committed to his work. But Lange, still a very young woman herself, had little patience for the girl. She taught Consie to cook, clean, sew, and iron, and (as Lange's grandmother had done) lashed out if the tasks weren't done exactly according to instructions. She became so frustrated with Consie that she'd often slap her. The two fought all the time. Lange would feel terrible after she exploded at the child and would beg Consie not to tell her father. This conflict continued throughout Lange's and Dixon's marriage, and Consie was sent for long periods of time to stay with close family friends, the Wilsons.

CHILDREN

On May 15, 1925, Lange gave birth to her first child, Daniel Rhodes Dixon. John Eaglefeather Dixon was born three years later, on June 12, 1928. She adored her children, but after their births her work and life began to change. There was never any question about who would assume responsibility for their day-to-day upbringing; Lange would tend to them and to all the household chores. She usually performed her chores in the morning, arranged for the boys' meals, and then went to her studio. Juggling work with her familial duties proved to be difficult, but she also viewed her business as crucial to the financial security of the family. Dixon and she believed that her studio enabled him to pursue his painting. When a newspaper reporter interviewed her about how she handled being married to an artist, Lange replied, "Simple. Simple, that is, when an artist's wife accepts the fact that she has to contend with many things other wives do not. She must first realize that her husband does not work solely to provide for his family. He works for the sake of his work—because of an inner necessity. To do both of these things successfully, he needs a certain amount of freedom—freedom from the petty, personal things of life. . . . As Maynard's wife, it is my chief job to see that his life does not become too involved—that he has a clear field." (Meltzer, 61) She didn't seem to have a problem then with living in Dixon's shadow.

Later on in life, Lange recalled about that era, "I continued to reserve a small portion of my life . . . and that was my photographic area. But the most of my life and the biggest part, the largest part of my energy, my deepest allegiances, were to Maynard's work and my children." (Partridge, 97)

But Dixon's and Lange's problems escalated with her increased responsibilities. As the years passed, Dixon continued to go away on his long sketching trips. Usually he'd say he'd be back in four to six weeks, but typically he spent at least four months away at a time. To keep her business going, Lange felt she had to place the children with other families for months. She sometimes left them with the Wilson family (whom Consie was living with), and other times they stayed with Lange's brother, Martin, who lived in nearby San Jose. This separation from her children pained her, but she felt

"Mother's Day, While We Were Living at Virginia St." **Although
she spent much of her time traveling and documenting the troubles
of American people, Lange seems to have enjoyed the domestic
side of life. This photograph stands in strong contrast to her
documentary work; it is light and almost whimsical. (The hand
belongs to John Dixon, Lange's son with Maynard Dixon.) In her
later years, Lange was able to explore domestic life even more fully.**

that it was necessary. And the couple had other difficulties, too. Lange and Consie were still not getting along, and Dixon, with his defiantly populist ideals, often teased Lange about what he considered her elitism.

Yet Lange managed to maintain an active clientele for her portrait studio, and her business was thriving. Late in the summer of 1929, business was going so well that she thought she could afford to take a vacation with the family. So she closed the studio, and she, Dixon, and the boys took a trip to the Sierra Nevada. Lange shot some pictures of the landscape and some of her sons in the natural environment.

Most of the personal photographs Lange had taken during these years were images of her children. These shots incorporated aspects of her professional portraiture, yet they responded to the children's spontaneity. Still, she did experiment with other subjects. For example, she snapped some shots of plants, perhaps influenced by the work of her friend Imogen Cunningham (Imogen's studies of plants were featured in an exhibition in Stuttgart in 1929). But Lange wasn't very happy with the results. After she spent time on a friend's estate in the mountains, where she made some photographs, she said, "I tried to photograph the young pine trees there and I tried to photograph some stumps, and I tried to photograph in the late afternoon the way the sunlight comes through some big-leafed plants with a horrible name, skunk cabbage, with big pale leaves and the afternoon sun showing all the veins. I tried to photograph those things because I like them. But I just couldn't do it." (Ohrm, 21)

One day during the Sierra Nevada trip, while Lange was enjoying some tranquil moments alone outside, she had something of an epiphany, spurred on by nature. She was contemplating some of her recent work involving landscapes and feeling demoralized, when she noticed a thunderstorm stirring. She explained years later to her son Daniel, "When it broke, there I was, sitting on a big rock and right in the middle of it, with the thunder bursting and the wind whistling, it came to me that what I had to do was to take pictures and concentrate upon people, only people, all kinds of people, people who paid me, and people who didn't." (Meltzer, 63) This realization represented a crucial turning point in Dorothea Lange's work.

Documentary
Photographer

1929–1935

Photography records the gamut of feelings written on the human face, the beauty of the earth and skies that man has inherited and the wealth and confusion man has created.
—Edward Steichen, quoted in *Time*, April 7, 1961

[The] benefit of seeing . . . can come only if you pause a while, extricate yourself from the maddening mob of quick impressions ceaselessly battering our lives, and look thoughtfully at a quiet image. . . . [T]he viewer must be willing to pause, to look again, to meditate.
—Dorothea Lange

When Lange and her family returned to San Francisco after their vacation in the Sierra Nevada, her life and her attitude toward her photographs began to undergo a transformation. She was gradually growing dissatisfied with her commercial portrait work and had made up her mind to make photographs that she considered more serious, although she wasn't exactly sure how she would go about it. She later said, when speaking about her portrait business, "I could have gone on with it, and enlarged it, and had a fairly secure living, a small personal business, had I not realized that it wasn't really what I wanted, not really. I had proved to myself that I could do it, and I enjoyed every portrait that I made in an individual way. . . . I wanted to work on a broader basis. . . . I was still sort of aware that there was a very large world out there that I had entered not too well." (Ohrm, 22)

And there was much happening in the larger world around her. On October 24, 1929, the stock market crashed, and the entire country was thrown into chaos. Banks failed, factories closed, and unemployment skyrocketed. (At the height of the Great Depression, in 1933, about 33 percent of the total workforce was unemployed.) The whole nation was in crisis. People couldn't afford to spend money the way they used to, even the wealthy, so Lange lost commissions and Dixon had difficulty selling paintings. And as their economic challenges mounted, the tension between the couple increased.

In the summer of 1931, Lange and Dixon purchased a secondhand "Model A" Ford, their first car, and the family drove to Taos, New Mexico. Lange said later, "We weren't there because of the Depression, but because Dixon wanted to paint and there was enough money to see us through. The outside world was full of uncertainty and unrest and trouble and we went and we stayed there." (Partridge, 33) So the two of them, along with Dan and John, found an old Mexican adobe house on a hill, with just two rooms and no plumbing or telephone.

IN TAOS

While Dixon painted, Lange occupied herself with such chores as cooking and pumping water from the well. This period was the most time the children had ever spent with their mother. They even bought a pony, and Daniel and John learned how to

Dixon, cowboy/artist. Lange's first husband, Maynard Dixon, at his easel around 1920. Dixon, usually seen smoking hand-rolled cigarettes and sporting cowboy outfits, was an intriguing juxtaposition to Lange, a bohemian photographer of the city. The two made a dynamic duo, though, and inspired and motivated each other in their respective careers.

ride. Lange took photographs occasionally, mostly of towns-people and children, yet her familial obligations prevented her from totally concentrating on her work. But every morning in Taos she would watch "this very sober, serious man driving with a purpose down the road." (Meltzer, 66) She thought he must be an artist, and soon found out that he was Paul Strand, a photographer whose work she had seen. She said, "It was the first time I had observed a person in my own trade who took his work that way. . . . He had private purposes that he was pursuing, and he was so methodical and so intent on it that he looked neither to the right nor left. . . . I didn't until then really know about photographers who went off for themselves." (Meltzer, 66)

She pondered all the time she spent caring for her children, tending to the chores, and helping her husband, and she became acutely aware of the difficulties facing the female artist. "I have to hesitate before I say that I was too busy. Maybe I kept myself too busy. But that thing that Paul Strand was able to do, I wasn't able to do. Women rarely can, unless they're not living a woman's life. I don't know whether I was temperamentally sufficiently mature at that time to have done it. . . . I photographed once in a while when I could, but just a little." (Meltzer, 67)

After six months in Taos, the winter arrived and they were all ready to go home. On their drive back, the family witnessed firsthand the terrible havoc the Great Depression wrought. Life in Taos somehow had seemed removed from the crisis that consumed the nation at large. They saw homeless men walking aimlessly along the roads and teenage boys who had been sent away by their own families to fend for themselves.

When they arrived back in San Francisco in 1932, Lange and Dixon made an extremely difficult decision. She recalled later that, coming back to California, "we were confronted with the terrors of the Depression. Not that we didn't have enough to eat, but everyone was so shocked and panicky. No one knew what was ahead." (Meltzer, 68) They placed the boys, then just four and seven years old, in a boarding school in nearby San Anselmo, and lived apart in their respective studios. Lange moved into hers (then located at 802 Montgomery Street), and Dixon into his about half a block away. They thought that this would help them economize—they'd save the expenses of renting a house and running a household. On weekends, Lange and Dixon visited the boys, often taking them for picnics in the countryside and target shooting. But the arrangement was painful for all of them. Lange later said, "This was very, very hard for me to do. Even now when I speak of it I feel the pain. I carry these things inside and it hurts me in the same spot that it did then." (Meltzer, 68)

Back in her studio, Lange couldn't help feeling the absence of her children. But the strain somehow fueled her work. "Although my mind was over in San Anselmo most of the time and I didn't like to be separated from the children, it drove me to work. And I worked then as I would not have done, I am sure, if I had gone back to my habitual life." (Meltzer, 69) Her personal anguish gave her even more empathy for the growing legions of homeless men that she saw wandering along the sidewalks right outside her studio door. She became very conscious that the "discrepancy between what I was working on . . . and what was going on in the street was more than I could assimilate." (Rosenblum, 172)

One fall day, as Lange was making proofs in her second-floor studio (a few clients could still afford such luxuries as portraits), she watched as an unemployed young man walked up the street. She said, "He came to the corner, stopped, and stood there a little while. Behind him were the waterfront and the wholesale districts; to his left was the financial district; ahead was Chinatown and the Hall of Justice; to his right the flophouses and the Barbary Coast. What was he to do? Which way was he to go?" (Heyman, 14)

"WHITE ANGEL BREADLINE"

Lange couldn't close her eyes to the social turmoil all around her. She was overwhelmed by the need to act. Near her studio, on Market Street, a woman named Lois Jordan had set up a soup kitchen/breadline to feed starving and out-of-work people. She was a working-class widow, nicknamed the White Angel. Lange said, "I looked down at the line as long as I could, and then one day I said to myself, 'I'd better make this happen.'" (Heyman, 24) She loaded her 3¼-by-4¼-inch Graflex camera and walked down to photograph the breadline.

Lange was a little nervous to go alone, and she didn't know what to expect, so she took her brother Martin along with her for protection. She set up her camera and took shots of some of the men eating stew and drinking weak coffee. Then she took several others of the breadline. She moved with trepidation at first. She said, "I wasn't accustomed to jostling about in groups of tormented, depressed and angry men, with a camera." (Partridge, 17) But then Lange recalled what she learned as a girl walking along New York City's Bowery. She summoned her "cloak of invisibility," her singular ability to blend in and remain unassuming.

Camera in hand, she neared an elderly man who was hunched over a railing. He was looking down at his clenched hands and holding a tin cup between his arms. He was unshaven and his mouth was turned down. Behind him was a line of men, most of them better dressed. (His hat was markedly more soiled and worn than many of their crisp hats; most of them appeared to be newly unemployed.) He was facing away from them. Touched by the scene, Lange took two photos of the man, from different angles and distances. He didn't look up.

Later, when she was asked what she had felt about what she saw before her, Lange said, "I can only say I knew I was looking at something. You know there are moments such as these when time stands still and all you do is hold your breath and hope it will wait for you. And you just hope you will have enough time to get it organized in a fraction of a second on that tiny piece of sensitive film. Sometimes you have an inner sense that you have encompassed the thing generally. You know then that you

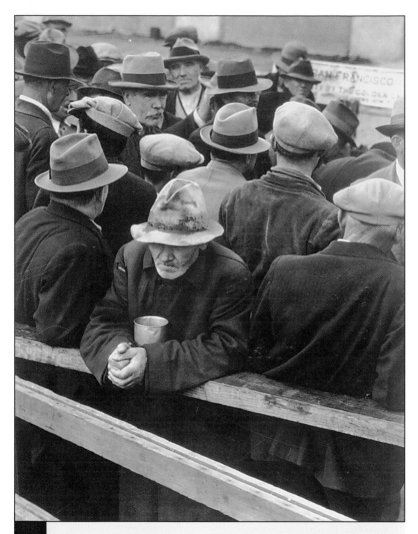

"White Angel Breadline." This photograph started Lange on her crusade to record the essence of people—"all kinds of people"— including those who had been ignored or forgotten by the rest of society. "White Angel Breadline" hung in Lange's studio for a long time as her inspiration for documenting the emotion and trauma of the Depression matured into a passion that would shape the rest of her career. "I had struggled a lot for months and months with this material," she said. ". . . But I saw something, and I encompassed it, and I had it."

are not taking anything away from anyone, their privacy, their dignity, their wholeness." (Ohrm, 24)

When she was done, she went back to her studio and developed the film in her darkroom. She also handed the film magazine holder to her assistant so he could reload it later, but she hadn't realized that a film was still inside. When her assistant discovered the film the next day, he developed it and brought it back to her. It was the photo of the man with the soiled, crinkled hat and the tin cup. She made a print of it and then examined it. She said, "I had struggled a lot for months and months with this material. . . . But I saw something, and I encompassed it, and I had it." (Ohrm, 24)

At the time, Lange didn't know what to do with the picture. She hung the image on the wall of her studio, interested to see how her customers would react to it. Most of them just glanced at or asked her, "What are you going to do with that sort of thing?" She had no idea, and she didn't know that this style and approach to photography would

"WHITE ANGEL BREADLINE"

This image is striking in that it reveals both the man's suffering and his dignity. It's discreet, and very noticeably made with respect and compassion. Lange took this shot from a higher angle, pointing the camera down toward the man. Compositionally speaking, he is at the center of a distinctly triangular shape formed by the rails against which he is leaning and the angled hats worn by the men behind him. His hat is one of the most prominent shapes in the image. The photograph eventually received nationwide recognition and praise. Titled "White Angel Breadline," it went on to become one of the most memorable images of Dorothea Lange's career and a classic photo of the Great Depression.

consume the next twenty years of her life. But she did know that she had to continue to photograph those people "who couldn't afford to pay her." She knew that she had to do more to show the human consequences and devastation of the Great Depression.

"PICTURES OF THE PEOPLE"

Lange became single-minded in her quest, entirely switching gears in her photographic work. She sent out to her studio clients a note declaring her intentions, that she was now a maker of "Pictures of People." She started taking her camera to more dangerous areas. At first, she was tentative with shooting these starving and often angry men, but she soon turned fearless. She took images of soup lines, and people sleeping outside in the streets, and makeshift camps.

She felt intense compassion for these people whose lives had been wholly disrupted by circumstances beyond their control. Perhaps she identified with them so strongly because she, too, knew what it was like to feel like an outsider. And her sympathy for the common man must have also been influenced by her husband's populist sensibilities, and probably, too, by the political beliefs of the new president, Franklin Delano Roosevelt (FDR).

FDR was inaugurated as president of the United States in early March of 1933. Like Lange, Roosevelt had contracted polio when he was a child, but he had lost the use of his legs as a result of the disease. The new president proposed a "New Deal," designed to rehabilitate the economy and provide relief for the country through government-sponsored programs. In a speech that he had delivered on April 7, 1932, he said, "These unhappy times call for the building of plans . . . that put their faith once more in the forgotten man at the bottom of the economic pyramid." (Partridge, 68) The phrase "Forgotten Man" had served as a defining part of FDR's campaign, and it became a motif in much of Dorothea Lange's work.

Under Roosevelt, Congress passed legislation that helped to ease the suffering of those affected by the Great Depression. In March of 1933, the Civilian Conservation Corp (CCC) was established. About 250,000 teenagers and young men were employed to do construction and conservation work. Their provisions included housing and meals, and they were paid about $30 a month. In May, Congress passed another law setting aside $500 million in aid to the Federal Emergency Relief Administration (FERA).

In 1934, as Lange spent more time photographing on the streets, she and Dixon once again tried to make their marriage work. Lange decided to give up her studio space, but she maintained her portrait business in their new house at 2515 Gough Street. (They moved Daniel and John back home with them, and the boys were thrilled.) Although Lange didn't really want to make portraits of the privileged anymore, the money from her business still helped fund Dixon's painting trips. She managed to keep her business afloat, though she had to continue the practice of placing the boys with other families. The boys hated being away from their parents, but Lange was committed to her photography.

Despite Roosevelt's sweeping, ambitious changes, millions of Americans remained unemployed. And many of those who were employed were paid extremely low wages and labored long hours. In May of 1934, the Longshoremen's Union went on strike at the docks. These were the men who loaded and unloaded the cargo from the ships that came into port in San Francisco. They were exhausted from their many hours of hard labor, which often meant 24- to 36-hour stretches. They wanted better wages and improved conditions. Lange took photos of them while they were striking, even though tensions were running high and people were, understandably, very angry and desperate. Once the strike began, the ship owners hired strike-breakers to transport the cargo, with the police protecting them as they worked. The situation turned violent, and hundreds of people were injured in the clashes. It culminated on July 5, 1934, known as Bloody Thursday. Governor Frank Merriam declared a state of riot and called in the National Guard, which sprayed tear gas and struck some of the men with clubs. In the end, two strikers were left dead. Laborers were furious and declared a general strike, throughout the city, on July 16.

Lange's photos of the strike were very different from those of other photographers. Many of the pictures in the newspapers featured shots of bloodied strikers and the violence. But Lange's images had more nuances. She always approached her subjects discreetly, and she seemed to be especially attentive to their gestures. Like the photos Lange had taken in the May Day demonstrations at San Francisco's Civic Center in 1933, her pictures often revealed something of their personality or state of mind through their hands, lips, or legs. ("Street Demonstration, San Francisco, 1933," a well-known photograph, featured a policeman facing a group of picketers; his feet are spread wide apart and his fingers are laced together over his belly, showing his authority.) Throughout her career, Lange was a keen observer of how powerfully the body reflects emotion and character traits.

One day in the summer of 1934, a friend of Lange's suggested that she exhibit some of the photos she had taken outside her studio. She had her first show at a small gallery in Oakland, in the studio of Willard Van Dyke, a well-known photographer who greatly admired Lange's work.

In a piece Van Dyke wrote for *Camera Craft*, he said, "[The people in Dorothea Lange's photos] are in the midst of great changes—contemporary problems are reflected on their faces, a tremendous drama is unfolding before them, and Dorothea Lange is photographing it through them. . . . She is not preoccupied with the philosophy behind the present conflict. She is making a record of it through the faces of the individuals most sensitive to it or most concerned in it. Her treatment of this type of human subjects shows her in turn

"Street Demonstration, San Francisco, 1933." One of Lange's many photographs of the 1933 May Day demonstrations in San Francisco. Lange always managed to capture a subject or moment's personality and emotion through simple or discreet gestures or movements. This piece shows the policeman asserting his authority over the situation by lacing his hands in front of him and adopting a strong stance.

sensitive and sympathetic to the uncertainty and unrest at the present time." (Heyman, 20)

Lange's way of photographing people, unposed in their natural surroundings, was nothing short of groundbreaking.

She was one of the earliest pioneers in the United States of a style of photography known as documentary photography. When explaining herself later as a documentary photographer, she said: "Hands off! I do not molest what I photograph, I do not meddle and I do not arrange." (Heyman, 16) Lange's photos are factual and unflinchingly direct. She said, "The documentary photograph carries with it another thing, a quality [in the subject] that the artist responds to. It is a photograph, which carries the full meaning of the episode or the circumstance or the situation that can only be revealed—because you can't really recapture it—by this other quality. There is no real warfare between the artist and the documentary photographer. He has to be both." (Meltzer, 84) Her photographs have an urgency to them, yet they also reveal astonishing emotional depth. She connected on a real level with her subjects and conveyed their suffering while revealing their resilience and perseverance, and, always, their dignity.

Some of Lange's photographer friends also were recording the drastic social changes occurring around them, but none of them did it with her high degree of determination and personal involvement. Some of them had joined together—including Imogen Cunningham, Edward Weston, Ansel Adams, Willard Van Dyke, and others—and called themselves "Group f64." They advocated what they called "straight photography"; this meant that they never manipulated their images in any way. The f64 movement was very progressive for the era. Although Lange counted many of the group's members as her friends, and she often discussed her work with them, she never exhibited her work with them. Ansel Adams said, "Although she did participate in a few informal discussions, I don't think she shared in our objectives." (Meltzer, 75) Lange ardently believed that her photographs had to fill a social need.

At the gallery show, Lange's photos were seen for the first time by lots of people. Viewers, unaccustomed to seeing such direct, blunt images of social protests, were amazed. Her work provoked strong responses. In fact, Van Dyke himself was so affected by her photos that he soon stopped working on still photography and moved east, eventually becoming a documentary filmmaker. But perhaps no viewer was quite so taken by Lange's work as Paul Schuster Taylor.

PAUL TAYLOR

Taylor, a sociologist and economist at the University of California, was so impressed with what he saw that he telephoned Lange and asked if he could use one of her images to illustrate an article he had worked on. He had written a piece on San Francisco's general strike for a magazine called *Survey Graphic*, a social-science magazine with a populist bent. Taylor was a New Deal progressive who specialized in agricultural issues and migratory labor. He thought her visuals would complement his text, and she agreed to let him use the picture. (The article, with her photo, was published in September 1934.)

Then, when Taylor was studying some of California's self-help cooperatives (small groups of unemployed people who exchanged their labor for supplies), he convinced Willard Van Dyke to invite some photographer friends to shoot one of the communities. That summer, Lange, Imogen Cunningham, Van Dyke, and Mary Jeanette Edwards ventured to Oroville in the Sierra foothills to photograph the Unemployed Exchange Association (UXA), a group of families that ran an old sawmill together. There, Lange and Paul Taylor met for the first time.

She admired how Taylor spoke to people at the UXA; he talked with them gently, unobtrusively, and casually, and his lack of presumption helped him to draw out honest personal observations from them. His understated manner never made them feel self-conscious. Lange said about this trip, "I knew about people going and asking questions and filling in questionnaires, but an interview I had never heard. And I was very interested in the way in which he got the broad answers to questions without people really realizing how much they

A collaborative documentary. In 1934–1935, Lange teamed up with the economist Paul Taylor to document the plight of California's migratory workers. Taylor felt it crucial to use Lange's subtle and poignant photography to complement the written report the government had requested of him. He felt Lange could adequately and appropriately capture the true grit and severity of the situation. Lange, similarly, was intrigued by the manner in which Taylor went about documenting the emotions of subjects through interviews and the written word. A lasting friendship was building that would eventually lead to marriage.

were telling him. Everybody else went to bed while he was still sitting there in that cold miserable place talking with these people." (Ohrm, 42)

Their statements made Taylor's studies more compelling, and they supported the larger issues he was addressing in his reports. And Taylor observed Lange with interest, too. He recalled later that the first thing he saw Lange do when she arrived at the site was photograph a man leaning on his ax and looking up at trees. He liked the fact that she chose an angle most other photographers wouldn't consider: She photographed the man from behind. He thought her work was subtler than that of other photographers.

In the winter of 1934–1935, California's federally funded State Emergency Relief Administration (established as part of Roosevelt's New Deal) asked Paul Taylor to create a report on the state's increasingly serious migratory labor problem. Indigent workers, numbering in the tens of thousands, were streaming into the state, looking for jobs. They were destitute and hungry. SERA needed to find out who these people were, where they came from, why they were in trouble, and what the government should do to remedy the situation.

Farmers across the United States were in terrible shape. The Depression had caused prices for cattle, pigs, and chickens to plunge, and crops were similarly affected. Plus, machines such as harvesters and tractors were eliminating the need for human labor. Then thousands of farmers from Kansas, Texas, Arkansas, Oklahoma, and New Mexico were forced to leave their farms because a terrible drought destroyed their crops. Their land was dried out, and fierce winds destroyed the topsoil. The area encompassing these states became known as the "Dust Bowl." Desperate, farmers migrated to California, hoping to find better conditions; but there were too many workers and not enough jobs.

Paul Taylor, well known for his studies on migratory labor, was the perfect choice to prepare the report. He agreed to work for SERA, part-time, as a consultant. He would study who came to California, why they were in distress, and determine how the state could best serve their needs. He would aim to make people aware of the dire living conditions suffered by migrants and believed that the government should sponsor emergency camps to help out the migrants. Taylor would gather statistics and compile data, but he thought his reports needed something to bring his words to life. He wanted Lange to take photos, so the administration could see how severe the situation was. He said, "My words won't be enough to show the conditions visually and accurately." (Meltzer, 94)

In the beginning of 1935, Lange joined Paul Taylor's staff, placed on the SERA payroll as a "typist" because no provision for a photographer had existed. Lange said later, "My papers were made out as a typist because they'd just roar back if you mentioned photographer." (Partridge, 50) She was able to procure photographic materials by calling them "office supplies."

In February that year, Lange placed the boys with some friends yet again and went to work with Taylor. They traveled to Nipomo for the pea harvest and then went down to Imperial Valley. Lange was shocked by what she saw.

The pair visited the makeshift camps set up by migrants, where she observed overcrowded huts, cobbled together with scraps of wood, canvas, twigs, and anything else the poor families could find. She saw how these workers and their families were forced to live in squalor and scrape together meals. They also desperately needed adequate clothing and had no access to clean water. Lange and Taylor worked tirelessly, and they found that they worked exceptionally well together. Taylor would interview people while Lange photographed. Another member of Taylor's team, Tom Vasey, recalled Lange's first days in the field: "She was a small person with a slight limp. The characteristic pose was with the Rollei on her left shoulder, held by her left hand. From here it always seemed least distracting to the subject as she brought it down for use after a bit of talk. She was particularly adept in getting close-up cooperation with the women and children." (Meltzer, 95)

As Lange had learned to do when she began her studio business, she used her extraordinary ability to make people feel at ease. She never used her camera to intrude on people's privacy, and she would never photograph people if they refused to be photographed. And, after watching and learning from Taylor, Lange was asking questions, too. She found that in the migrant camps "they were always talkers. This was very helpful to me, and I think it was helpful to them. It gave us a chance to meet on common ground—something a photographer like myself must find if he's going to do good work." (Meltzer, 97)

Together, Taylor and Lange gathered the information they thought they needed to convince the government to establish sanitary camps for the families. They made a great team. Clark Kerr, a young social scientist working with them in California's Central Valley in 1934, recalled that they had "complementary skills but contrasting personalities. She was always moving, mostly talking, reacting in a flash, living in the moment," whereas "Paul thought carefully about everything, spoke seldom, and then softly." (Partridge, 39)

The Taylor–Lange reports were scientifically driven documents, complete with Taylor's carefully collected statistical figures, detailed analyses of the conditions they witnessed, and compelling quotes from the migrant workers. Lange's photographs were powerful, and they provided the ideal visual counterpart to Taylor's writing. Their reports—scientific information combined with compassionate and moving photography—became the paradigm for similar documentary projects for decades to come.

The Taylor–Lange reports were read in the SERA office, where they were well received, then handed on to the Federal Emergency Relief Administration in Washington, D.C. Lange and Taylor's efforts persuaded the government to build sanitary camps where the migrant families could live while they harvested the crops. FERA immediately gave SERA $20,000 to construct the first two emergency migrant camps in California, in Marysville and Arvin. The camps provided tent platforms, stoves, toilets, and a community building.

Dorothea Lange was realizing that her photographs not only could document human suffering but also ultimately help alleviate it. Her work played a major role in changing thousands of people's lives.

6

Documenting the Depression

1935–1940

I think the best pictures are often on the edges of any situation. I don't find photographing the situation nearly as interesting as photographing the edges.

—William Albert Allard

Photography is a major force in explaining man to man.

—Edward Steichen,
quoted in *Time*, April 7, 1961

By the spring of 1935, Lange and Taylor's professional relationship had grown, and their personal relationship had intensified, too. They spent more time together out in the field, traveling all around California, interviewing and photographing the migrants. While on assignment in the Imperial Valley, Lange came to a realization: She was deeply in love with Paul Taylor. Her marriage to Dixon had been troubled for years, and she

76

found Taylor to be an attractive man of great integrity. She admired the tenacity with which he stood by his convictions, and she found him to be a solid and loyal man. Taylor, too, was in love with Lange. He had tremendous respect for her, and his marriage to Katherine Page Whiteside had also been failing. Taylor and Lange divorced their respective spouses, both mostly amicably, and were married on December 6, 1935, in Albuquerque, New Mexico.

Taylor had three children from his first marriage—Katherine, thirteen; Ross, ten; and Margot, six—and his wife left them with him while she worked on her doctorate in New York City. So Taylor, Lange, Daniel, John, and the three Taylor kids all moved into a redwood, two-story house on Virginia Street in Berkeley. It sat over a canyon, and the family had beautiful views of the San Francisco Bay in the distance. Lange continued to struggle with the conflicting demands of family and work, and again sent the children to stay with three different families while she worked away from home for stretches. She would often spend her week out in the field, but on weekends she and Taylor tried to gather the kids together at their home. Of course, the children weren't very pleased with living away from them. And even when she was with them, Lange was very picky about maintaining an orderly, pristine household. The kids never knew what to expect from her—she was a perfectionist, and she could get angry suddenly and quickly, as she had done earlier with Constance Dixon. And Taylor always deferred to Lange, even if the target of her rage was one of his own children. The children loved her, but they also feared her, even nicknaming her "Dictator Dot."

Lange, now forty years old, felt more committed to her work than ever. She closed down her portrait studio operations and became totally devoted to documenting the serious social changes that were happening all around her. Lange had a strong sense of mission. The country was in the midst of a major transformation. The nation was shifting from an agriculture-based

Dictator Dot. At home, Lange ran a tight ship, and her children affectionately nicknamed her Dictator Dot. In the field, though, Lange believed in getting to know her subjects and becoming comfortable with them before making a photograph. Lange's free spirit and her person-first methodology enabled her to shoot some of the nation's most insightful photographs.

society to an industrialized one, and she wanted to record how it affected the people who were caught up most directly in the turmoil. When she was in Imperial Valley, on the same trip on which she realized she would marry Taylor, Lange witnessed this event:

> There was a car full of people, a family there at that gas station. . . . They looked very woebegone to me. They

were American whites. . . . I looked at the license plate. . . . [I]t was Oklahoma. . . . I approached them and asked something about which way they were going, were they looking for work. . . . And they said, "We've been blown out" . . . and then they told me about the dust storm. They were the first arrivals that I saw. All of that day, driving for the next . . . three or four hundred miles, I saw those people. And I couldn't wait. I photographed it. I had those first ones. That was the beginning of the first day of the landslide that cut this continent. (Heyman, 24)

The Great Depression had tarnished almost every sector of the American economy, but the farming industry felt the biggest impact. The massive western migration across the United States, which had started in the 1920s when farm prices were driven down and farmers were forced into poverty, was gaining even more momentum. As the Depression wore on, farmers had to flee their homes, pushed out by drought and dust storms. Between 1935 and 1940, more than a million people left their farms and headed for California. These people were called Okies, short for Oklahomans, though they came from many other states as well.

Lange photographed the Okies, but she also was becoming interested in other types of migrants. As she learned more about California's labor history, she began to investigate the racism that was so ingrained in the system. She photographed Mexican migrants, black pickers, and Filipinos laboring in the fields.

Lange's work was taking on new urgency and broadening in scope. Now she could channel her enthusiasm and passion into a new project—one that she'd participate in for several years and that would bring her nationwide attention and praise.

Roy Stryker, the head of the Historical Section of FDR's newly created Resettlement Administration (RA) in Washington, D.C., had noticed Lange's photographs in the

Taylor–Lange reports. He was so affected by them that he had her transferred immediately from the SERA to the RA, on September 1, 1935. Ben Shahn, another photographer who worked for Stryker, recalled that he was present when Stryker first saw Lange's work. Shahn said, "This was a revelation . . . what this woman was doing." (Meltzer, 104) Her title was now "Photographer-Investigator," and she'd earn about $2,300 a year. Around that same time, Paul Taylor was appointed regional labor adviser to the RA, assigned to the same office as Lange.

The Resettlement Administration (eventually renamed the Farm Security Administration, or FSA) had been established to provide financial relief and aid to the rural populations devastated by the Great Depression. Their programs included soil conservation projects, experimental communal farms, loans that enabled farmers to purchase good land at low interest rates, and, of course, sanitary camps for migrant farm workers. As head of the Historical Section, Stryker and his staff were to record anything of historical importance to the RA/FSA. His goal was to help the RA/FSA receive financial support from Congress; he needed to show Americans how desperate rural America's situation was so more money would be set aside to ease the suffering of the families.

STRYKER'S FSA

As soon as Stryker arrived in Washington, he began assembling a talented team of photographers. By the end of that year, his photographic staff included Lange, Arthur Rothstein, Shahn, Walker Evans, and Carl Mydans. In addition, Esther Bubley, Pauline Ehrlich, Russell Lee, Gordon Parks, Marion Post Wolcott, Jack Delano, and Jon Collier, Jr. would all eventually work for the RA/FSA at some point during its existence.

The photographers were supposed to document images of the plight of farm families across the country, but Stryker saw that he had an opportunity to oversee something unprecedented—a sweeping visual examination of the United States. He instructed his staff to shoot as much as they could—of both the landscape and its people. They were creating a record of the Great Depression, but the end result was the most highly acclaimed photographic collection ever compiled in the United States. By 1942, Stryker's staff had taken more than 270,000 photographs of the country.

When Stryker gave his photographers their assignments, he would first brief them, then provide background material, including maps, pamphlets, and economic, historical, and sociological studies about the region they were covering. Then he sometimes drafted "shooting scripts." The photographers would be sent out on shooting trips, usually lasting months at a time. Stryker would write them long assessments about the work they were sending him and about additional photos he needed. (These letters were especially significant in Lange's case, since she was based on the West Coast.) Then the

ROY STRYKER

Roy Stryker had been an economics instructor at Columbia University in New York City before he was assigned to the RA/FSA post. He had handled the photography research for *American Economic Life and the Means of Its Improvement* (1925), a book written by Rexford Tugwell, Stryker's mentor at Columbia who became the head of the new Resettlement Administration. Through his research on the book, Stryker had become familiar with the work of Jacob Riis and Lewis Hine, two early photographers who used their cameras to encourage social reform. So Stryker was well aware of photography's ability to effect change, and he had been using photographs in his economics classes for years. He had the experience and sensibility to recognize the power of Lange's work.

"Ross Taylor When Young, Ten Years Old." This photograph was taken in 1935, when Lange's relationship with Paul Taylor was becoming a potent force in her life. (She married Taylor later in that same year.) Lange herself later described the picture: "This is that special photograph, which reveals the boy, at that particular time. Which was a hard one for him. But shows the drive and sharp sense of direction, also the anger. How he threw those rocks—"

photographers would develop their film, draft brief accompanying text, and post the materials back to Stryker's office to be edited, printed, and published.

Although sometimes the shooting scripts listed specific RA-sponsored projects Stryker wanted his staff to shoot, Lange recalled that, more often, "You were turned loose in a region, and the assignment was more like this: 'See what is really there. What does it look like, what does it feel like? What actually is the human condition?'" (Partridge, 111) Stryker wanted his photographers to develop their own ideas as they went along and construct their own themes out of those ideas.

Stryker trusted Lange's artistic sense implicitly. She would set out on field trips using his general suggestions, but without a specific plan of what to shoot. She and Taylor both believed that their best work came from experiences that were unplanned and unexpected. The job with the RA granted Lange a lot of freedom, and it was, in many ways, ideal for her; she could express both her artistry and her social activism. She had the following to say when she first visited the RA offices:

> I found a little office, tucked away, in a hot, muggy early summer, where nobody especially knew exactly what he was going to do or how he was going to do it. And this is no criticism, because you walked into an atmo-sphere of a very special kind of freedom; anyone who tells you anything else and dresses us up in official light is not truthful, because it wasn't that way. That free-dom that there was, where you found your own way, without criticism from anyone, was special. That was germane to that project. That's the thing that is almost impossible to duplicate or find. (Partridge, 18)

But Lange had difficulties with Stryker. Although the two had enormous respect for each other's artistic sense, their long-distance relationship was fraught with conflict. They were always professional with one another in their correspondence, but tension simmered beneath the surface. Each was stubborn in his or her own way. The biggest source of the frustration between them was the issue of Lange's negatives. Lange wanted to print them herself, but Stryker required his staff to send their rolls of film to the D.C. office as soon they were exposed. Lange couldn't see the pictures themselves until weeks later, after they had been printed by government employees.

Since her photographs were considered government property, Lange had to ask to borrow a negative from the D.C. office when a museum or publisher wanted to reprint one of her images. When she first asked the agency to loan her a negative for a major exhibit, she was told that they would make the print for her instead. But Lange wanted to see the print herself. She said, "This show is the most important photographic show we have. It tours the country. It tours Europe. I couldn't afford to show prints, unsigned, which I have never seen. I'll send the negative right back." (Partridge, 20) And she wanted to keep her negatives as a personal record of her work. She said to Stryker, "It is not too much for a photographer to ask that he have one set of proofs, if only to have some sort of record of what he has been doing. It guides him, in how the work is building up, whether or not it is taking form." (Ohrm, 101)

Lange and Stryker continued to clash about the issue of her negatives for the duration of her time on the RA/FSA payroll. (And, eventually, this conflict would contribute to her being permanently cut from the FSA roster at the end of 1939.)

IN THE FIELD

One of Lange's first assignments for the RA, at the end of 1935, was documenting how the emergency sanitary camps she and Taylor had helped to establish were actually aiding the migrant families. The migrants in the new camps paid just a dollar a week, and they were given access to showers, toilets, stoves, and tents, and they could even gather together in a central recreation hall. If the family had no money at all, its members could work in exchange for services and food.

Lange and Taylor promoted the establishment of these camps throughout the country. Lange took pictures of the migrants cooking and washing in the camps, of nurses working with some ill children, and of people talking and playing music. She wanted to show the government and the country how the camps had improved the lives of the families. But

Dorothea in the field, 1938. Lange had an uncanny ability to put a subject at ease and record the essence of that subject's being in that moment in time. She especially was able to gain the cooperation of women and young children, like this young boy in a migrant worker camp. Her policy was to make sure her subjects knew *her* before she asked anything about *them*. She even allowed children to play with her cameras, believing that generosity on her part would lead to generosity on theirs.

many nonmigrants were against the camps from the beginning. They didn't want the migrants' children going to school with their kids, and they objected to the migrants' getting free medical care. Others were afraid that the migrant workers would gather together in the recreation hall, form a coalition, and demand higher pay.

In the early months of 1936, Lange carried on her investigation into migrant conditions in California. Occasionally,

Ron Partridge, the teenage son of Imogen Cunningham and Roi Partridge, would accompany her on trips and act as her assistant. Typically, Lange would simply go out in the general direction of her assignment and drive until she saw something that drew her. And she always tried to go in with an open mind. As Willard Van Dyke wrote in *Camera Craft,* "Her method is to eradicate from her mind before she starts, all ideas which she might hold regarding the situation—her mind like an unexposed film." (Van Dyke, 461)

Ron Partridge described: "I'd be going twenty miles an hour and she'd say, 'Slow down, Ron, slow down.' Her eyes would go from one side to another, taking in every little thing. When we saw something—a broken car, a camp of migrants, a farm machine, a field boss—we would stop." (Partridge, 59) The sights they saw always moved her. Migrant workers set up small shantytowns along rivers or irrigation ditches, constructing shelters with anything they could find, like cardboard, tin, twigs, or grass. The makeshift camps were overcrowded and filthy, and there was never enough food, and what the people ate usually lacked any nutritional value. There weren't any facilities, so people would go to the bathroom in the fields, and they'd bathe in the same places where they got their water. Many of the children were sick with stomachaches and diarrhea, due to their poor diets and the unsanitary conditions.

Lange did whatever she could to make the people she photographed comfortable with her and her camera. Some-times she'd sit on the ground and let the children touch the camera. She said, "You let them because you know that if you behave in a generous manner you're very apt to receive it . . . and I have told everything about myself long before I asked any questions." (Partridge, 59) Lange felt that just speaking and spending time with them was what she needed to do. "So often it's just sticking around and remaining there, not swooping in and swooping out in a cloud of dust," she said. Lange explained to some of them that the government wanted a record of what was happening so they could help. She also believed that her limp made people feel that she, too, knew what it was like to suffer and to feel like an outsider. "It gets you off on a different level than if you go into a situation whole and secure. . . . My lameness as a child and acceptance finally of my lameness, truly opened gates for me." (Partridge, 59)

When she felt that she had gained their trust, Lange would set up either her Rolleiflex or her 4-by-5-inch Graflex, which she mounted on a tripod. Lange liked working with these large-format cameras and wide-angle lenses. Even though these cameras were larger and clunkier than the 35-millimeter cameras other photographers were using, she preferred them because of the interesting angles she could achieve. She held her Rolleiflex at her waist, not at eye level as a 35-millimeter camera would be held. This allowed her to look up at the people she shot, and this perspective seemed to bring out her subjects' strength, even heroism. Those qualities were highlighted by the vast expanse of sky behind them. Regardless of how much the people suffered, Lange always recognized and revealed their determination and spirit.

After shooting, Lange would go back to her car to write down some of what her subjects said to her. When Ron Partridge was with her, they each selected one subject and focused on what that person had said. They searched their memories for every possible detail; then each wrote down what he or she remembered and shared it with the other to create as complete a story as possible.

Lange had remarkable instinct and an uncanny ability to be in the right place at the right time. On a cold, wet evening in March of 1936, that rare talent helped her create the most famous image made by anyone on the RA/FSA staff, and one of the most widely praised and reproduced photos in all of American photography.

"MIGRANT MOTHER"

Lange was driving back to San Francisco alone one night in the rain when she passed a sign that read "Pea Pickers Camp." She was utterly exhausted—she'd been on a grueling schedule, photographing migrant workers for a month—so she didn't want to stop. "I didn't want to stop and I didn't," Lange later said. But twenty miles later, a strong feeling seized her. She felt compelled to return to that camp. "Almost without realizing what I was doing I made a U-turn on the empty highway. . . . I was following instinct, not reason; I drove into that wet and soggy camp and parked my car like a homing pigeon." She walked straight over to a distressed and desperate-looking woman, who was surrounded by her hungry and dirty children. She said she was drawn to the woman "like a magnet." (Ohrm, 19)

Lange found out that the woman was 32 and had seven children and that her family had been surviving on the peas that had frozen in the surrounding fields and birds that her children had killed. The family was stranded because she had sold tires from her car to buy food. Lange spent just about ten minutes photographing the woman. She took six shots, and with each shot she moved in closer. Lange said that the woman "seemed to know that my pictures might help her, and so she helped me. There was sort of an equality about it." Although there were many other stranded pea pickers in the nearby tents and huts, Lange took no other photographs that evening. She said, "I knew I had recorded the essence of my assignment." (Meltzer, 132–133)

When she got home, she developed her film and went straight to the city editor of *The San Francisco News.* She told him that the pea pickers in Nipomo were starving. The editor quickly passed on the news to the United Press. The headline of the March 10, 1936 edition of the *News* declared "Food Rushed to Starving Farm Colony." The U.S. government quickly shipped twenty thousand pounds of food to the migrants.

The Okie migration. Midwestern farmers, termed "Okies" because so many were from Oklahoma, came to California by the hundreds of thousands in the late 1930s, seeking employment after years of crop failure and drought. Lange was there to capture their movement and, more importantly, how their movement affected them, their families, their way of life, and their hope for the future. It was Lange's work, with the work of other RA/FSA photographers, that drew public attention to the plight of migrant workers.

Although "Migrant Mother" didn't accompany the article, two of Lange's other images did. The famous migrant photo was first published in *The San Francisco News* and *Survey Graphic*.

The "Migrant Mother" photo was soon reprinted and exhibited again and again in newspapers across the country. It's easy to see why the photo caused such a ruckus. Although

Lange connected purely with the woman, the photograph she created seemed to capture the suffering of an entire country, while at the same time conveying its indomitable spirit. The mother is looking off into the distance; her hand is close to her mouth, showing her worry and concern. Her children are hiding their heads and leaning on her. The baby sleeping in her lap is filthy. It is an astonishing, powerful, and deeply compassionate image.

ON THE ROAD

The photo also was exhibited five years later at the Museum of Modern Art in New York City, and it became the quintessential photograph of the era. It was so widely seen and famous that Lange started to insist, "I am not a 'one-picture' photographer." (Meltzer, 136) Lange wanted to be known for more than having taken just "Migrant Mother."

After Lange completed the trip that culminated in "Migrant Mother," she traveled to Utah to photograph some RA rehabilitation projects. Later that spring, Paul Taylor was transferred to the Social Security Board, and in May he and Lange made a trip east to Washington to meet with Roy Stryker for the first time. There she also met some of her colleagues, including Ben Shahn and Arthur Rothstein.

From Washington, Lange went to New Jersey, where she documented the Hightstown project. New York City garment workers had lost their jobs when the Great Depression hit. The Hightstown project aimed to resettle families of those workers on four hundred acres in New Jersey. Lange photographed the people in their homes in New York City slums and also in the area where they worked in Manhattan.

In the summer, Taylor and Lange headed for the South, where they would study tenancy, another one of the RA's most significant concerns. The Washington, D.C. office had received countless requests from magazines and newspapers for more photos on the subject.

Company housing. Lange photographed these shacks, company housing in a small town in Utah, in March of 1936. One of her missions with the Resettlement Administration was to document the living conditions in shantytowns like this one, as well as in the emergency migrant camps she herself had helped to establish. Although many Americans were against the formation of the FSA's camps, Lange worked to demonstrate through her photographs how the camps drastically improved the lives of thousands of destitute laborers.

Lange had spent most of her time with the RA/FSA studying the families that had left their homes, but she and Taylor now turned their attention to the ones that stayed behind. Farmers in the South and Southwest were hit hard by the Depression, but the sharecropping system that had been in place long before had left millions of farmers, both white and black, in poverty. At the time, up to 75 percent of all farms in the South were operated by tenant farmers. Tenant farmers and sharecroppers raised crops on land they didn't own. They either paid their rent in cash or gave 50 percent of their harvests to their landlords, who in many cases were direct descendants of plantation owners. They couldn't afford to buy their own tools, seed, or farm animals, so they had to borrow from those who could. They almost never earned enough to pay them back, so they often were stuck in a miserable cycle of poverty.

Lange and Taylor traveled first to North Carolina, where she shot poor white laborers hoeing crops. They then went to Birmingham, Alabama, where she photographed some iron and steel mills. Right down the road, Lange and Taylor spoke with an African-American tenant family of seven. They said that they only earned $150 a year for the combined labor of the adults and all five children. When they stopped in Georgia, they encountered peach pickers who said they earned just 75 cents a day.

Soon Taylor and Lange made their way to the Delta, where she took several photographs of African Americans praying. In July, in northwestern Mississippi, she and Taylor visited Dixie Plantation, an RA project. They found that the tenant farmers there had been cheated by the RA agent, just as private plantation owners had been cheating sharecroppers and tenants elsewhere. Lange sent a long letter to Washington reporting this travesty.

But Lange always found and photographed extraordinary people and places, too. In Arkansas, they spent time at a fascinating place. A socialist minister named Sherwood Eddy founded a cooperative whose members raised cotton and ran a sawmill and a poultry farm. What made this place so interesting was that it was integrated, with blacks and whites working and

Racism in the Deep South. As Lange moved from photographing California's migrant workers to documenting the Depression's effect on the Southern states, she ran into strict racial segregation and anti-black prejudice. This photograph of a white plantation owner and his farm hands clearly demonstrates this sentiment. The well-fed white man's presence with his status symbol—an automobile—dominates the piece. It towers over the poorer, slim workers, whom he reduces by turning his back on them.

living harmoniously in the same community. The Deep South that Lange and Taylor had been studying was deeply segregated, so this cooperative was truly inspiring. Lange photographed the members working and learning side by side, and blacks and whites celebrating together.

One of Lange's most famous photographs was taken around this time, in nearby Clarksdale, Mississippi. It seems to symbolize the rampant racism that pervaded the Deep South at the time. The photo features a white plantation owner in the foreground presiding over black field hands who are probably patrons of his store. Lange shot this from a low angle, so the white man is clearly dominating the scene. His hand is placed proudly and confidently on his knee and his body is leaning possessively into his shiny automobile, a symbol of his power and wealth.

Then Lange and Taylor headed west, through Oklahoma and Texas, ultimately arriving back in California at the end of August. In October, the Historic Section of the RA was in trouble, and Lange received some bad news. Due to drastic budget cuts, she was dropped from the payroll. Although she and Stryker continued to have their misunderstandings, and her geographical distance from Washington was a source of bureaucratic difficulty for him, he respected her ideas and her work immensely. So in January of 1937, she was hired back, and she immediately got to work on the Lubin report, a Senate document on migratory labor.

Life in the field was sometimes dangerous. In February, Lange wanted to return to the Imperial Valley, which at the time was teeming with displaced and angry migrant workers. Lange wrote in a letter to Stryker that "people continue to pour in and there is no way to stop them and no work when they get there."

She wrote, "Down there it is too uncomfortable to be alone," and she said that she was taking Ron Partridge to accompany her. "If the vigilantes and Associated Farmers don't like you they shoot at you and give you the works. Beat you up and throw you into a ditch at the county line." (Heyman, 28) But she and Ron went, photographing from morning until evening, staying in cheap cabins all along the way.

BACK TO THE SOUTH

In May of 1937, Lange and Taylor set off for another extended trip through the South. They took Taylor's twelve-year-old son along with them and drove south through California's rural valleys, then into Arizona, where they encountered more migrants searching for work. They met a family who had lost two babies to typhoid. They talked to families in New Mexico and farmers in Texas.

As Lange and Taylor met more people, they were discovering that the mass exodus of farmers was the result not only of drought, dust storms, and crop failure, but also of the gradual mechanization of agriculture. In a letter she wrote to Stryker in June, Lange said that in Childress and Hall Counties in Texas she found "people put off farms, tenants, often of years standing and established—with tractors coming in purchased by the landowners with Soil Conservation money. Not just a few cases. It's the story of the county. The ex-tenants are homeless and landless. How far across Texas the same story holds we do not yet know." (Ohrm, 76)

Lange and Taylor found that mechanized farming was forcing farmers out and putting them on relief. A group of seven young tenant farmers in Hardeman County, Texas told Lange and Taylor that they were all on WPA relief, trying to support their families on $22.80 a month. Although the men were hesitant at first, they eventually talked for a while. Lange, in her usual manner, recorded some snippets of their conversation—"The landlord on this place bought a tractor and put five families of renters off," for example, or "He has two families on day labor, at from 75 cents to $1.25 a day." They all felt hopeless and powerless. "If we fight, who we gonna whup?" (Ohrm, 78) Lange photographed these men, standing in a row in front of a house, and it was another especially striking and memorable shot.

Lange said later, "What I see now is the mechanization has brought about enormous problems. There is no place for people to go to live on the land any more. . . . We have, in my lifetime, changed from rural to urban. In my lifetime, that little space, this tremendous thing has happened." (Partridge, 114)

Lange and Taylor moved through Arkansas and Mississippi,

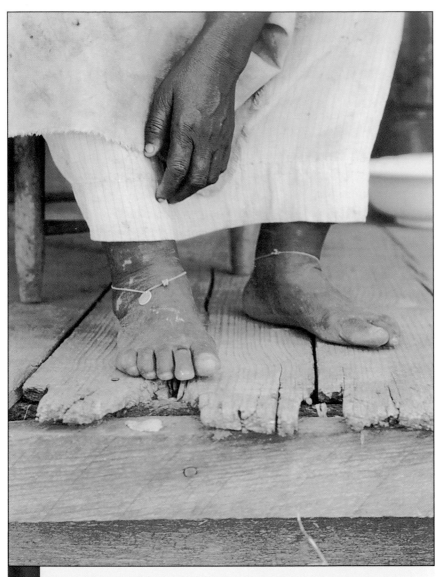

The feet of a sharecropper. Lange had an affinity for the details and nuances of people. This photograph suggests the hardships of the Southern sharecroppers by focusing simply on an elderly woman's scarred and shoeless feet. It was by capturing details such as these that Lange and the other FSA photographers hoped to deliver the "bigger picture" of the working poor.

seeing both refugees of the drought and "tractor refugees."
(Meltzer, 176) She made all sorts of portraits of a wide variety
of Southern people—children, elderly people, ex-slaves, poor
white tenant farmers, and plantation owners. She seemed to
have a particular sympathy for black farmers. She photographed emaciated fieldworkers and ramshackle homes with
collapsing roofs. She continued to train her eyes on small
gestures, and on such details as their worn hands and feet,
weathered skin, and ragged clothing. "Sharecroppers" (1937)
shows an African-American family hoeing the land.

Lange and Taylor had by that time established an effective
way of working together. While they were visiting an ex-slave
living in Texas, Lange photographed while Taylor spoke with
the man about his childhood as a slave. Taylor said that he
would usually start a conversation with his subject, and then
"out of the corner of my eye, I would see that [Lange] had got
out her camera, so I would just keep the talk going. I had
their attention. . . . Keeping out of range [of the camera]
generally wasn't a problem. She worked pretty close to them
for the most part. If I thought I was interfering I would
just sidle out of her way as inconspicuously as possible,
talking to them all the time. My purpose was to make it a
natural relationship, and take as much of their attention
as I conveniently could, leaving her the maximum freedom
to do what she wanted." (Ohrm, 57)

As Lange was working in the Deep South, she asked
Stryker if she should concentrate on white farmers. Stryker
advised her to "Take both black and white but place the
emphasis on the white tenants, since we know that these will
receive much wider use." (Heyman, 28) And after the RA had
been transferred to the FSA earlier that May (and put under
the jurisdiction of the Department of Agriculture), Stryker
wanted his staff to photograph not only poor families, but to
widen their focus to include more positive aspects of rural
life. This wasn't difficult for Lange, as she always found

hopeful places or people, wherever she went. He specifically wanted them to document the culture of small-town American life before it disappeared entirely. Lange took some photographs of North Carolina parishioners cleaning their church. She took images of schools, grocery stores, and street corners where farmers congregated. And she photographed some more government-established communities. For instance, she went back to Hill House in Mississippi, and she also snapped shots of people on their way to found the Matanuska settlement all the way up in Alaska.

At the end of 1937, Lange again was cut from the FSA payroll due to budget difficulties. But she concentrated on working on her own projects, traveling throughout California, the West, and back into the South in 1938, until she was rehired by Stryker in September. In 1939 she visited the Northwest and North Carolina, and she did yet more work in California. Still, she and Stryker continued to disagree about the control of her negatives, and there were other problems, too. Stryker was furious when Lange hired her friend Ansel Adams to make some prints of her work for the Museum of Modern Art; he didn't like her using working documents as art. While he never questioned the quality and integrity of Lange's work, he found her to be demanding and difficult to work with. In January 1, 1940, Lange was dropped by the FSA for the last time. "I had to get rid of one photographer and I got rid of the least cooperative one," he said. (Partridge, 22)

Lange was terribly hurt by this. Although many of her colleagues at the FSA protested her firing, and friends wrote letters on her behalf, reminding Stryker of how much Lange and Taylor had done for migrants, she was never reinstated.

At the end of the FSA project, Stryker was asked what he believed was the greatest lesson to be learned from the massive collection of photographs his staff had created. He answered, "Dignity versus despair. I believe dignity wins out." Perhaps more so than any of the other FSA photographers, Dorothea Lange understood this sentiment and reflected it in her work. Even Roy Stryker had said that, of all the work produced by his staff, Lange "had the most sensitivity and the most rapport with people." (Meltzer, 104)

Minorities
and the War
1940–1956

In America, the photographer is not simply the person who records the
past, but the one who invents it.
— Susan Sontag, *On Photography* (1977)

All photographs are accurate. None of them is the truth.
— Photographer Richard Avedon

During her last few years with the FSA, Lange, together with
Taylor, began to compile *An American Exodus: A Record of Human
Erosion*. This was an expansion of the ideas they had developed
while working in the field. *American Exodus* was one of a few
books of the Depression era that blended text and pictures to
depict the sweeping social and economic changes that cut across
rural America. Many of Lange's pictures also had been used in
Land of the Free, a "collection of photographs illustrated by a
poem" written by Archibald MacLeish. (Meltzer, 184)

Lange in 1937. The love of photography dominated every phase of Lange's adult life. As life took its twists and turns around her—from social upheaval and economic collapse to ups and downs in her personal life—Lange returned again and again to her camera to find her voice. The 1940s and 1950s marked the start of a series of new projects for her; she photographed in shipyards and in Ireland and, perhaps most importantly, documented the anti-Japanese racism that surged in the United States after Pearl Harbor.

American Exodus examined how slavery, tenancy, and the invention of the cotton gin caused the depopulation of the rural South and West, and how the steady migration to California was linked to a nationwide crisis. What set this book apart from others of the period was that the subjects' direct quotations formed the foundation of the text. Lange said, "So far as possible we have let them speak to you face to face." (Ohrm, 112) But *American Exodus* was not well received by the American public at the time of its publication in fall 1939. German forces were tearing through Europe, and Americans were losing interest in the plight of migrants and the Great Depression. They now turned their full attention to what their role would be in World War II.

Yet Lange's FSA photographs were reaching a wider audience and garnering more acclaim. Some of her work was used as part of an FSA exhibit in New York City, and she had a major portfolio in *U.S. Camera.* Lange achieved another milestone in 1940, when "Migrant Mother" was displayed at the Museum of Modern Art in Manhattan. And in March of 1941, she became the first female photographer to win the prestigious Guggenheim Fellowship. (She also was the third photographer ever to receive the scholarship.) This opportunity provided her with the funds to begin her next project: Lange hoped to photograph some cooperative religious settlements in the West, including the Mormons in Utah, the Hutterites in South Dakota, and the Amana Society in Iowa, but when the Japanese bombed Pearl Harbor, Hawaii, on December 7, her work on that series came to an abrupt end. A new chapter in her career was beginning.

THE RELOCATION OF JAPANESE-AMERICANS

Before Japanese forces bombed the American naval base in Pearl Harbor, Americans had been hesitant about entering the war. Yet when their country was attacked on their own soil, most citizens rallied behind President Roosevelt and his declaration of war on Japan and its allies, Germany and Italy. But the U.S. government and many Americans were afraid that the Japanese would invade the Pacific Coast. And they believed that the Japanese-Americans living on the coast might be spies who would help plan the attack. Anti-Japanese sentiment spread, and it soon ballooned into hysteria. Many Japanese-Americans, to prove that they were loyal to the United States, even burned their photos of ancient Japanese relatives and other symbols of their Japanese heritage. Still, on February 19, 1942, President Roosevelt issued Executive Order #9066, which called for all people of Japanese descent living on the West Coast—110,000 men, women, and children—to be moved to detention camps for the remainder of the war. Lange and Taylor were adamantly against this measure, believing that the Japanese-Americans were victims of prejudice, stripped of their civil rights simply because of their racial background.

Even though Lange was outspoken about her opposition to the evacuation, the War Relocation Administration (WRA) hired her to document it. The work that she completed for the WRA—760 photographs in all—is some of the most humane and poignant of her career, but it quietly evoked her outrage, too. And her images, as usual, revealed Lange's tremendous respect for her subjects. Lange took pictures of the evacuees from April through September of 1942. She spent time with them as they packed their belongings and closed their businesses. She snapped shots of them while they were registering with the government, and she photographed the children in schools. She went to bus stations and train stations with them and then accompanied them to temporary assembly centers. (One of these was located at an old racetrack, and detainees were held in stalls in which horses used to be kept.) When the detainees were moved to permanent centers a few months later, Lange continued to record their activity.

Most Americans at the time supported the relocation of the Japanese-Americans, so Lange and Taylor were in the minority. (In the spring of 1942, Taylor published one of the first articles sympathetic to the Japanese-American detainees

Executive Order #9066: Japanese-American relocation. Adamantly opposed to the forced government relocation of Japanese-Americans during World War II, but paid to document it, Lange was determined to do some good in this new phase of her career. Working for the War Relocation Administration (WRA), she recorded what she felt was a blatant violation of human and civil rights on film. The results were some of the most deeply personal works of her career. This photograph was taken in San Francisco on April 6, 1942, as Japanese-Americans assembled for relocation to an assembly center camp. Lange can be seen in the background with her camera.

to appear in a national magazine.) Lange was horrified by what was happening. Christina Gardner, who accompanied Lange on several shoots, said that one night in May 1942, "Dorothea was in some sort of paroxysm of fear. . . . She realized that this was such an erosion of civil liberties, she had gotten so consumed by it and realized the import of it so heartily that it was something that I cannot explain to this day." (Partridge, 50)

By December of 1945, all the camps except one were closed. But many of the Japanese-Americans returned to find themselves with no homes or businesses. Forty years later, the government issued an apology and gave $20,000 to each surviving Japanese-American who had been detained during the war. Lange's photographs for the WRA weren't released officially to the American public until 1972.

RICHMOND SHIPYARDS

When Lange wrapped up her work for the WRA, she began taking pictures of various minority groups working on the West Coast. Hired by the Office of War Information (OWI), she photographed Mexican-Americans, Italian-Americans, African-Americans, and Hispanic-Americans, among others.

MANZANAR DETENTION CAMP

Lange took three trips to Manzanar, a detention camp in Owens Valley, California. Located in the middle of the barren, desolate desert, the camp was surrounded by armed guards and high barbed wire. Lange recalled the visits years later with a kind of national remorse: "They had the meanest dust storms there, and not a blade of grass, and the springs are so cruel; when those people arrived there they couldn't keep the tar paper on the shacks. Oh, my. There were some pretty terrible chapters of that history. . . . I was employed a year and a half to do that, and it was very, very difficult. This is what we did. How did it happen? How could we?" (Partridge, 121) At Manzanar, Lange, who always was accompanied by armed guards, photographed the people in the stuffy, uncomfortable barracks and in the long lines waiting to eat in the dining hall. Other photographers had been assigned to record this event, including Lange's friend Ansel Adams, but none of them so reflected the unfairness and inhumanity of the situation in their work.

Many of these pictures appeared in OWI publications abroad. Then she and Ansel Adams were employed by the magazine *Fortune* to record 24 hours in the lives of workers at the Richmond shipyards, a place that created job opportunities for thousands of ex-migrant farmers, African-Americans, and women when the war started. The small industrial town was booming. Before the war, Richmond had a population of about twenty thousand; in 1944, more than one hundred thousand people were employed at the yards. (Among those working in the yards were Lange's brother, Martin, who was a foreman, and her son, Daniel.)

Lange and Adams worked in entirely different ways. Adams arrived at the yards loaded with equipment; Lange just brought her usual Rolleiflex camera and notebook. Adams, who created beautiful panoramic vistas of the West, took the wider view, photographing the grander aspects of the huge shipyards. Lange quietly insinuated herself into the crowd, focusing, in her typical way, on individuals and details. Christina Gardner said of Lange's method in the yards, "She had a peculiar facility for just melting away and for not seeming to be photographing at the same time that she was sticking a camera in somebody's face. People ignored the camera's presence for her." (Meltzer, 249)

In addition to taking pictures of workers in the yards themselves, Lange also took her camera into the workers' neighborhoods. She photographed the lively main streets and laughing children. Adams and Lange labored on this project from early morning until late at night, and they found that they worked very well together.

But all this time, Lange was suffering from increasingly poor health. In the early years of the war, she had developed severe stomach pains, often accompanied by vomiting and nausea. Additionally, she was worried about her son, Daniel, then twenty years old. He had quit his job at the shipyards and seemed to be drifting about, unsure of what to do with his life.

"One Nation Indivisible," April 6, 1942. Lange's work with the WRA took her into the personal lives of Japanese-Americans, where she discovered an astonishing degree of loyalty and patriotism in a dispossessed and misunderstood people. This photograph of Japanese-American schoolchildren reciting the Pledge of Allegiance suggests Lange's opinion of the blindness and intolerance that the U.S. government and the American people were showing toward their fellow countrymen.

He joined the army, but that didn't ease his inner turmoil, as he was often absent without leave (AWOL). In August, when Lange had finished documenting the founding of the United Nations in San Francisco, her illness took a turn for the worse. She was hospitalized and had her gall bladder removed, but she continued to experience intense pain. (It was later found out that the doctors had misdiagnosed her; she actually had stomach ulcers.) Lange was so consumed by the pain and the frequent hospitalizations over the following years that she stopped actively photographing until around 1950.

BACK TO WORK

Lange's battle with her ailing stomach persisted, and at one point she hemorrhaged so severely that she nearly died. For long periods of time she was too depleted and aching to work at all; but slowly she started using her camera again. She photographed the graduation at the University of California—Berkeley in 1950, and she shot James Roosevelt's campaign for California governor. She also started photographing her family more. In 1951, Lange's first grandchild, Gregor Dixon, was born to her son John. And there was more good news: After an especially difficult period—during which he had been discharged from the Army, had been homeless for some time, and had been banned from the Taylor–Lange household following heated arguments—Dan had decided he wanted to be a writer. He wrote his first article for *Modern Photography*. It was a piece about Lange, accompanied by her images.

In 1953 Lange felt healthy enough to commit herself wholeheartedly to photography again. She went back to Utah, finally resuming the investigation that she had started before the war, but this time she was with Ansel Adams and accompanied by her son Daniel. They produced a photo essay for *Life* titled "Three Mormon Towns." Adams shot landscapes, while Lange photographed the people in the villages of Gunlock, St. George, and Toquerville.

In 1954, Lange and Daniel traveled to Ireland to complete another photo essay for *Life,* this one called "The Irish Country People." Lange had been inspired to produce this piece after she read *The Irish Countryman,* a book by the anthropologist Conrad N. Arensberg. She wanted to capture the people of County Clare, as she was intrigued by their strong connection to the land and to Irish customs. She also began two other pieces for the magazine. In "The Public Defender," she followed the quest of a young lawyer, Martin Pulich, to defend people who couldn't afford to pay for their own legal services. Although *Life* ultimately did not use her work, in time her

"The Irish Country People," 1954. **Inspired by Conrad Arensberg's *The Irish Countryman* (1937), Lange traveled to County Clare with Daniel Dixon to document the life of Irish farming communities. Her work was published as a photographic essay in the popular magazine *Life* later in the year.**

photos from that series were seen in several newspapers and other publications. "Death of a Valley," created in 1956 with her photographer friend Pirkle Jones, examined a rural community in California that was being destroyed by the creation of the federally funded Berryessa Dam.

Lange was in her sixties during the "Death of a Valley" project, and her health was slowly deteriorating, but her commitment to making photographs with an eye toward social justice was as strong as ever.

8

Grandmother and World Traveler

1956–1965

Pick a theme and work it to exhaustion. . . . [T]he subject must be something you truly love or truly hate.

—Dorothea Lange

No place is boring, if you've had a good night's sleep and have a pocket full of unexposed film.

—Robert Adams

In 1955, Taylor and Lange acquired a little wooden cabin on California's coast in a place called Steep Ravine. Although it was a very small, rustic two-room structure, it became the center of their family life. One room was a living room and kitchen area; the other was a bedroom. As Lange's health declined, she turned more and more to her family, especially the grand-children, who became her favorite photographic subjects. "[Steep Ravine] became our special place to be together, and to

110

Paul Taylor carrying Lisa. As Lange's health deteriorated, she began to settle more into family life. In 1955, she and Taylor acquired Steep Ravine, a two-room cabin on California's coast where she could focus on her favorite new photographic subject: her grandchildren. Some have suggested that the affection she lavished on the grandchildren was an atonement for the attention she had not given to her own sons—that once the initial intensity of photography was past, she could relax into the role.

be with the children." (Meltzer, 310) Her camera lens was now trained on the tender gestures of the small children, friendships between family members, and intimate moments shared with close friends.

There was no electricity, no phone, and no hot water at Steep Ravine, but Lange's grandchildren, and many of her extended family (including Ron Partridge's children), thought the place was magical. In the cold months, the children would help gather firewood while Lange prepared meals and tended to the outside chores. At night, by the light of kerosene lamps and warmed by the heat of the fireplace and the wood-burning stove, they played Parcheesi, or Taylor read to the children. Often Dee Taylor played her flute or Greg Dixon his clarinet. During the day, Lange took the kids for walks along the beach, always with her camera in hand. One friend of Lange's remembered watching Lange collecting driftwood with one of her grandchildren: "I thought how she was giving this child the time and attention her own boys did not get from her. When she was starting out as a photographer, she was so intense about her work she could not give the children what they needed. It's taken for granted that a man has to go off and do his work. Lange knew that, of course. Still, I think she felt guilty about what she had done—or not done—and was atoning for it with the next generation." (Meltzer, 10)

TRAVELING ABROAD

In 1958, Paul Taylor started working as a consulting economist for the U.S. government and other private foundations. He advised officials in poor countries about such issues as health and agriculture. He was most interested in community development, figuring out ways that members of the community could work together to address concerns like sanitation and family planning. Although he had taken other trips by himself, Taylor knew that a journey he had planned through Asia would keep him away for at least six months, so he wanted Lange to accompany him.

Lange wasn't very excited about the prospect of leaving her grandchildren behind for so long. And she also worried about the state of her health. But when she asked her doctor, "Should I go?" he replied, "What's the difference whether you die here or there? Go!" (Partridge, 130)

So Lange and Taylor left for Asia in June of 1958. Lange had no specific agenda for her photography during this trip; she simply shot whatever caught her eye. During their eight-week stay in Korea, she photographed people in the city streets and the country. She was particularly drawn to the children; one series of photographs focuses on the eyes of some Korean children. Lange took an extremely close-up shot of the face of a young Korean boy; the photo is cropped to reveal his innocence. His face is rounded, with a wide forehead and closed eyes.

Still, she found it difficult to work in Asia. She said, "I cannot go out into the streets unaccompanied. I am surrounded, my clothes examined, my hair stroked. I am a novelty, and the camera just tops it off." (Meltzer, 320) She was often frustrated, but she still managed to make some inspired pictures. She photographed a man walking on his hands down the street in Saigon and shot three generations of a family planting onions near Panmunjom. In Bali, she found it easier to photograph, as the Balinese people didn't seem to pay much attention to the tourists. There she photographed dancers, honing in on their legs and hands. She also visited Japan, Indonesia, Thailand, Nepal, Singapore, India, and Pakistan.

Lange often was overwhelmed by the misery and variety of what she saw in Asia. She said, "The tropics, and it may be Asia, cannot be photographed on black and white film. I am confronted with doubts as to what I can grasp and record on this journey. The pageant is vast, the pageant is vast, and I clutch at tiny details, inadequate." (Partridge, 132)

In 1960, Taylor was hired by the United Nations to study some community development programs in South America. So he and Lange took another trip, spending two months in Ecuador and Venezuela. As always, Lange loved observing, discovering, and learning about the different cultures and peoples she saw, but she missed home, and she was feeling weaker and weaker.

In 1961–1962, Lange was in very poor health, spending much of the year in the hospital. But her work continued to gain more exposure and considerable praise. She was a nationally known photographer, and she was lauded internationally as

"Two Women." This curiously titled image was made in Nepal in 1958, during Lange's trip through Asia with Paul Taylor. Just as she had done in the 1930s in the United States, Lange strolled through the streets of the areas she visited, creating scores of "street scenes," such as this one, that capture both the subject and the subject's world. Lange attributed her success in this medium to her "cloak of invisibility," which may really have been a talent for putting people at ease.

well. Lange's photographs were included in the Museum of Modern Art's FSA survey, titled "The Bitter Years." Her work also was seen in *Aperture*, and exhibits at the San Francisco Museum of Art, the Art Institute of Chicago, and galleries in Boston, Louisville, and France and Italy.

Lange and Taylor took their last trip abroad together in 1963. She met up with Taylor in Alexandria, Egypt, where he was a visiting professor at the university. She photographed now and then, finding it difficult to work in Alexandria. She was surrounded by crowds, followed by begging children, and often harassed. She thought Alexandria was "a dirty, crowded, noisy place with the splendor gone. The narrow streets and alleys are filled with people buying selling pushing hauling arguing squatting eating sewing hammering hawking their wares and drinking their delicious sweet black coffee out of dirty glasses." (Meltzer, 334) But she still made some beautiful photographs in Egypt, and she often found pleasure

> looking quietly and intently at living human beings going about their work and duties and occupations and activities as though they were spread before us for our pleasure and interest. A huge opera. A huge arena. And also to be only dimly self-aware, a figure who is part of it all, though only watching and watching. This is an exercise in vision, and no finger exercise, either. For a photographer it may be closer to the final performance. (Meltzer, 335)

After a long trip into the desert, where she encountered some enchanting images for her photographs, Lange contracted dysentery. She lost so much weight that she had to hold her clothes up with safety pins. She also had trouble sleeping. She felt like she was gradually getting better—but then, one night in June, during a trip to Iran, Taylor was awakened by her moaning and incoherent speech. He took her temperature; she was running a fever of 103°F. She was seriously ill, so they flew to Switzerland, where they learned that she had malaria. She recuperated for three weeks at a hospital where she felt very well cared for, and her condition slowly improved. But their travels were over, and they finally flew home in September.

DOROTHEA LANGE'S LAST DAYS

In August of 1964, Lange, her immediate family, extended family, and her vast network of friends received some devastating news. She wrote to a friend, "In the last two weeks time has stood still. I now know that I shall not recover as I have been able to so many times before, for I have an inoperable and incurable cancer of the esophagus, and the way ahead is unchartable." (Partridge, 107)

Lange was terribly sick; her diagnosis was definitive. Although she was tempted to recover quietly and perhaps return to the hospital in Switzerland where she had received such excellent care, she opted instead to plunge into her work. The photographic director of the Museum of Modern Art, John Szarkowski, had wanted to exhibit a retrospective of Lange's work. This would cover a lifetime of her photography. It was an ambitious, daunting project, and for the first time in her life, Lange had access to almost all her FSA work. She said, "I'm now faced with a really tremendous and dangerous job. I would very much like to avoid it. On the other hand, I feel I must do it." (Partridge, 107)

LANGE AND THE HOLIDAYS

The holidays were a particularly special time for Lange. Regardless of the nature or the number of projects she was involved in, every year she would stop her own work before Thanksgiving and not resume until after the Christmas season. This was a time she kept just for family, and she spent weeks preparing for the festivities. Lange's famous Thanksgiving celebrations typically included Dan Dixon, his wife, Mia, and their daughter; John Dixon, his wife, Helen, and their children; Ross Taylor, his wife, Onnie, and their children (Margot and Katherine had moved back East with their husbands); Roi Partridge and his whole family; and many other friends from faraway places. The Thanksgiving gathering was an elaborate, joyful affair that culminated in Paul Taylor's ceremonial reading of Abraham Lincoln's Thanksgiving Proclamation of 1863. Lange's meals were delicious and beautifully presented. She was just as meticulous and careful with these preparations as she was with her photographic work.

So, helped by many of her friends, family, and colleagues, Lange got straight to work reviewing her career output and developing themes for the show. Szarkowski flew out, and the two of them concentrated on selecting two hundred images for the show. Then she pored over all of her field and travel notes to cull material she could use for drafting captions. She became obsessive about her work in her final months. On top of this enormous undertaking, she was also the subject of interviews and two documentary films about her life and career. And she finished a collection of portraits of American rural women as well. (The book was not published until 1967, after her death). She once said, "I'm always pushing in many directions at once, always trying to overreach myself. It keeps me constantly restless, and probing and fractured. . . . However that way of working engenders a very good kind of fatigue, because it keeps you alive. You may be exhausted by the complexities of your existence, but there is no retreat in it. You are right out on the thin edge all the time, where you are unprotected and defenseless."(Partridge, 134)

And Lange worked almost right up to her last breath. A few days before she died, she saw the first prints for her retrospective. While she was in the hospital and knew she was dying, she said to Taylor, "This is the right time. Isn't it a miracle that comes at the right time?" (Partridge, 111)

Lange died peacefully on October 11, 1965, surrounded by her family.

The tiny woman from Hoboken, who walked with a limp and rose to the top of her field when few other women worked outside of the home, had become one of the premier American photographers of the twentieth century. Once called the "greatest documentary photographer in the United States" by Edward Steichen, Dorothea Lange was a pioneer in socially committed photography. Her work remains a lasting tribute to the power and resilience of the American spirit.

1895 Dorothea Margaretta Nutzhorn is born in Hoboken, New Jersey, on May 25.

1902 Contracts polio, resulting in a lifelong limp.

1907 Father, Henry Nutzhorn, abandons the family; Dorothea and her younger brother Henry, along with their mother, Joanna, move in with their grandmother in Hoboken.

1907–1909 Attends school at P.S. 62 in the Lower East Side of Manhattan; feels lonely and isolated at home and in school; pores over books and observes city life; develops her "cloak of invisibility," an ability to blend in without attracting attention.

1910–1913 Attends Wadleigh High School in Manhattan; spends much of her time cutting classes and wandering around New York City.

1913–1914 After graduation from high school, announces her intention of becoming a photographer; at her mother's insistence, enrolls at the New York Training School for Teachers; works in portrait studios around Manhattan, including that of Arnold Genthe.

1915–1917 Works in the studios of Aram Kazanjian and A. Spencer-Beatty; attends a photography class taught by Clarence H. White at Columbia University.

1918 With childhood friend Fronsie, leaves New York City to travel around the world; after they are robbed in San Francisco, the two decide to stay and work there; Lange works at the photo-finishing counter at Marsh's, joins a camera club, and befriends Imogen Cunningham, Roi Partridge, and other artists.

1919 Opens her own portrait studio at 540 Sutter Street; drops her father's name and assumes her mother's, Lange; meets Western wilderness painter Maynard Dixon.

1920   Is married to Maynard Dixon on March 21.

1922–1923   Travels with Dixon to the Southwest on two separate occasions; Dixon paints while Lange photographs.

1925   First child, Daniel Dixon, is born on May 15; Lange maintains an active clientele for her studio while raising her family.

1928   Second son, John Dixon, is born on June 12.

1929   Travels with family to the Sierra Nevada in California; returns with family in the fall, just after the stock market crash of October 24.

1931   Travels with family to Taos, New Mexico; lives there for several months; photographs while Dixon paints.

1932   The Dixons return from Taos; decides with Dixon to save money by living in their respective studios and placing the boys in a nearby boarding school; unsatisfied by her studio work, Lange takes her camera into the streets and creates "White Angel Breadline" and other pictures of people affected by the Great Depression.

1934   Photographs the general strike in San Francisco and exhibits her work for the first time, at Willard Van Dyke's studio; Paul S. Taylor, a respected economics professor, notices her work and uses one of her images to accompany an article for *Survey Graphic*.

1935   Joins Paul Taylor's staff at California's State Relief Administration; photographs destitute migrant farmers throughout California. The Taylor–Lange reports successfully convince the government to establish sanitary camps for the migrants. Impressed by Lange's work, Roy Stryker, the new head of the Resettlement Administration (RA) in Washington, D.C., has her transferred from the SERA to the RA. Lange divorces Maynard Dixon and marries Taylor in December.

1936 Photographs migrants in California; makes "Migrant Mother" in March and travels to Washington to meet Stryker for the first time; investigates the South with Taylor, studying tenancy; is dropped from the RA payroll in October due to budgetary cuts.

1937 Is rehired by Stryker in January; travels with Taylor through the South and the Southwest, where Lange photographs sharecroppers, tenant farmers, and Okies. The RA is renamed the Farm Security Administration (FSA), and at the end of year Lange is cut from the payroll again.

1938 Works on her own, photographing in California and the South; Stryker rehires her in September.

1939 Photographs more in California, then in the Northwest and North Carolina; *American Exodus*, a collaboration between Taylor and Lange, is published at the end of the year.

1940 Is permanently dropped from the FSA rolls; "Migrant Mother" is displayed at the Museum of Modern Art (MOMA) in New York City.

1941 Becomes the first female photographer to win the prestigious Guggenheim Fellowship; begins photographing religious settlements in the West but does not finish the project.

1942 Photographs Japanese-American detainees for the War Relocation Authority.

1943–1945 Photographs minority groups for the Office of War Information; collaborates with Ansel Adams on a piece for *Fortune* on the Richmond shipyards.

1946–1951 Photographs the founding of the United Nations in San Francisco; stops actively photographing due to stomach illness; some of her images are included in MOMA's "Sixty Prints by Six Women Photographers" in 1949.

1953–1956 Lange and Ansel Adams, assisted by Lange's son Daniel, produce "Three Mormon Towns" for *Life*; Lange and Daniel travel to Ireland to photograph "The Irish Country People," also for *Life*; Lange works on "The Public Defender" and "Death of a Valley," a collaboration with Pirkle Jones, for the same magazine, although the editors ultimately do not use Lange's photographs.

1958–1960 Accompanies Taylor through Asia, Europe, and South America, photographing intermittently.

1961–1962 Spends months in the hospital; her work is included in MOMA's survey of FSA photography, "The Bitter Years," and in galleries in Chicago, Boston, Louisville, and San Francisco and also in France and Italy; Lange photographs her family and friends around her beloved cabin in Steep Ravine, California.

1963 Travels through Egypt with Taylor, photographing occasionally; contracts dysentery and malaria; after recuperating in Switzerland, returns home in September.

1964 In August, is diagnosed with inoperable cancer of the esophagus; works with John Szarkowski, director of photography at MOMA, in selecting photographs for a retrospective of her work.

1965 Completes a collection of portraits of American rural women, published posthumously as *Dorothea Lange Looks at the American Country Woman* (1967). On October 11, Dorothea Lange dies.

Works by Dorothea Lange

As Published in Books

Dorothea Lange: Farm Security Administration Photographs, 1935–1939. Text-Fiche Press, 1980.

Dorothea Lange Looks at the American Country Woman. Amon Carter Museum at Fort Worth and Ward Ritchie Press, 1967.

Dorothea Lange: Photographs of a Lifetime. Essay by Robert Coles. Aperture, 1982.

Dorothea Lange's Ireland. Text by Gerry Mullins; essay by Daniel Dixon. Roberts Rinehart Publishers, 1998.

Lange, Dorothea, and Ansel Adams. "Three Mormon Towns." *Life,* September 6, 1954, pp. 91–100.

Lange, Dorothea, and Margaretta Mitchell. *To a Cabin.* Grossman, 1973.

Lange, Dorothea, and Paul Schuster Taylor. *An American Exodus: A Record of Human Erosion.* Reprinted from 1939 edition. Arno Press, 1975.

Lange, Dorothea, and Pirkle Jones. "Death of a Valley." *Aperture,* 1960, Volume 8:3, pp. 5–11.

Photographing the Second Gold Rush: Dorothea Lange and the Bay Area at War, 1941–1945. Introduction by Charles Wollenberg. Heyday Books, 1995.

The Photographs of Dorothea Lange. Text by Keith Davis. Hallmark Cards in association with Abrams, 1995.

Collections

Farm Security Administration Collection, Prints and Photographs Division, Library of Congress, Washington, D.C.

The Dorothea Lange Collection, Oakland Museum, Oakland, California.

Bibliography

Adler, Bill, ed. *The Unknown Wisdom of Jacqueline Kennedy Onassis.* Citadel, 1994.

Heyman, Therese Thau. *Celebrating a Collection: The Work of Dorothea Lange.* Oakland Museum, 1978.

Meltzer, Milton. *Dorothea Lange: A Photographer's Life.* Farrar Strauss Giroux, 1978.

Ohrm, Karin Becker. *Dorothea Lange and the Documentary Tradition.* Louisiana State University Press, 1980.

Partridge, Elizabeth, ed. *Dorothea Lange: A Visual Life.* Smithsonian Institution Press, 1994.

Rosenblum, Naomi. *A History of Women Photographers.* New York: Abbeville, 2000.

Van Dyke, Willard. "The Photographs of Dorothea Lange: A Critical Analysis." *Camera Craft,* October 1934, Volume 41, pp. 461–467.

Further Reading

Books

Borhan, Pierre. *Dorothea Lange: The Heart and Mind of a Photographer.* Bulfinch, 2002.

Browne, Turner, and Elaine Partnow. *Macmillan Biographical Encyclopedia of Photographic Artists and Innovators.* Macmillan, 1983.

Dixon, Daniel. "Dorothea Lange." *Modern Photography,* December 1952, Volume 16, pp. 68–77, 138–141.

Dorothea Lange: American Photographs. Essays by Sandra Philips, John Szarkowski, Therese Thau Heyman. Chronicle Books, 1994.

Fisher, Andrea. *Let Us Now Praise Famous Women: Women Photographers for the U.S. Government 1935 to 1944.* Pandora Press, 1987.

Hirsch, Robert. *Seizing the Light: A History of Photography.* McGraw-Hill, 2000.

Lange, Dorothea, and Daniel Dixon. "Photographing the Familiar." *Aperture,* 1952, Volume 1:2, pp. 4–15.

Partridge, Elizabeth. *Restless Spirit: The Life and Work of Dorothea Lange.* Puffin Books, 1998

Riess, Susan. *The Making of a Documentary Photographer.* University of California, Bancroft Library, 1968.

Sandler, Martin W. *Against the Odds: Women Pioneers in the First Hundred Years of Photography.* Rizzoli, 2002.

Turner, Robyn Montana. *Dorothea Lange.* Little Brown, 1994.

Websites

Library of Congress—American Memory Collection: America From the Great Depression to World War II, Black and White Photographs From the FSA-OWI, 1935–1945
memory.loc.gov/ammem/fsahtml/fahome.html

Library of Congress—Dorothea Lange's "Migrant Mother" Photographs in the Farm Security Administration Collection: An Overview
www.loc.gov/rr/print/128_migm.html

The Oakland Museum of California: The Dorothea Lange Collection
www.museumca.org/global/art/collections_dorothea_lange.html

Index of Online Resources for Dorothea Lange's Photographs maintained by Artcyclopedia
www.artcyclopedia.com/artists/lange

Interview with Dorothea Lange, conducted by Richard K. Doud for the
Archives of American Art, Smithsonian Institution
artarchives.si.edu/oralhist/lange64.htm

Dorothea Lange: Photographer of the People
www.dorothea-lange.org

Index

Index

Index

page:

13: Library of Congress, digital ID
3c289444u

18: Library of Congress, digital ID
3b41800u

21: Credit unknown, photo courtesy
Elizabeth Partridge

24: © CORBIS

29: © Museum of the City of NY/CORBIS

33: © Rondal Partridge and Elizabeth W.
Partridge

36: Library of Congress, LC-USZ62-118636

42: © Stapleton Collection/CORBIS

45: Credit unknown, photo courtesy
Elizabeth Partridge

49: © The Dorothea Lange Collection,
Oakland Museum of California, City
of Oakland. Gift of Paul S. Taylor

55: © The Dorothea Lange Collection,
Oakland Museum of California, City
of Oakland. Gift of Paul S. Taylor

60: © The Dorothea Lange Collection,
Oakland Museum of California, City
of Oakland. Gift of Paul S. Taylor

64: © The Dorothea Lange Collection,
Oakland Museum of California, City
of Oakland. Gift of Paul S. Taylor

69: © The Dorothea Lange Collection,
Oakland Museum of California, City
of Oakland. Gift of Paul S. Taylor

72: © Imogen Cunningham Trust

78: © Rondal Partridge and Elizabeth W.
Partridge

82: © The Dorothea Lange Collection,
Oakland Museum of California, City
of Oakland. Gift of Paul S. Taylor

85: © Rondal Partridge and Elizabeth W.
Partridge

89: Library of Congress,
LC-USF34-009870-E

91: Library of Congress,
LC-USF34-009043-E

93: Library of Congress,
LC-USF34-T01-009599-C

96: Library of Congress,
LC-USF34-017111-C

101: © Rondal Partridge and Elizabeth W.
Partridge

104: Library of Congress, LC-USZ62-56704

107: Library of Congress, LC-USZ62-17124

109: © The Dorothea Lange Collection,
Oakland Museum of California, City
of Oakland. Gift of Paul S. Taylor

111: © The Dorothea Lange Collection,
Oakland Museum of California, City
of Oakland. Gift of Paul S. Taylor

114: © The Dorothea Lange Collection,
Oakland Museum of California, City
of Oakland. Gift of Paul S. Taylor

Cover: © The Dorothea Lange Collection, Oakland Museum of California, City
of Oakland. Gift of Paul S. Taylor

Contributors

Kerry Acker is a freelance writer and editor based in Brooklyn, New York. Some of her other books include Chelsea House's MAJOR WORLD LEADERS: *Jimmy Carter* and WOMEN IN THE ARTS: *Nina Simone.*

Congresswoman Betty McCollum (Minnesota, Fourth District) is the second woman from Minnesota ever to have been elected to Congress. Since the start of her first term of office in 2000, she has worked diligently to protect the environment and to expand access to health care, and she has been an especially strong supporter of education and women's health care. She holds several prominent positions in the House Democratic Caucus and enjoys the rare distinction of serving on three House Committees at once. In 2001, she was appointed to represent the House Democrats on the National Council on the Arts, the advisory board of the National Endowment for the Arts.